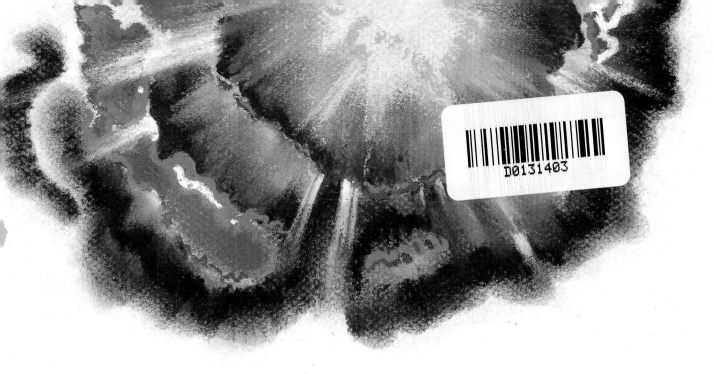

OUR UNIVERSE

A GUIDE TO WHAT'S OUT THERE

Russell Stannard

Kingfisher

NEW YORK

✱✱

Illustrators
Michael Bennallack-Hart
with Helen Floate (cartoons) and
Diana Mayo (atoms, balloons, and grapefruit)

Designers
Karin Ambrose and David Anstey

Typesetter
Tracey McNerney

Editor
Camilla Hallinan

KINGFISHER
Larousse Kingfisher Chambers Inc.
95 Madison Avenue
New York, New York 10016

First American edition, 1995
2 4 6 8 10 9 7 5 3 1

Text copyright © Russell Stannard 1995
Illustrations copyright © Larousse plc 1995

LIBRARY OF CONGRESS CATALOGING-IN-PUBLICATION DATA
Stannard, Russell.
Our universe: A guide to what's out there/
written by Russell Stannard: illustrated by Michael Bennallack-Hart.
—1st American ed.
p. cm.
Includes Index
1. Cosmology—Juvenile literature. 2. Astronomy—Juvenile literature.
[1. Stannard, Russell. Bennallack-Hart, Michael, ill.
III. Title.
QB983. S73 1995
520—dc20 94-32142 CIP AC

ISBN 1-85697-551-7

Printed in Spain

the Earthling, the Professor, and the Alien

✱✱

·Contents·

LEAVING HOME

Whenever you see a word in **heavy type**, you can check what it means in the glossary at the back of the book.

Come with me on a journey, to the farthest depths of space, and to the very beginning and end of time. I shall show you the **universe**.

There are so many strange and wonderful things to understand, so many mysteries to unravel—not only about the universe, but also about ourselves and our place in the world.

What do we need for the trip? Imagination. There's no other way to make this journey. No spaceship ever built (or ever likely to be built) can take us where we wish to go. But even though the trip has to be an imaginary one, scientists are fairly sure this is what such a journey would be like...

JUST A MINUTE!

Before we blast off into space, let's think for a moment. The Earth we live on is part of the universe we wish to explore. Except for the **Moon**, and possibly the nearby **planets**, it is the only part of the universe we can actually get our hands on. The laws of nature that rule everything going on here might be the same laws that apply everywhere else. So why not take a quick look around here on Earth, before we launch out into the unknown?

ROUND OR FLAT?

First of all, there is the shape of the Earth. Long ago, everyone thought the Earth was flat—apart from the odd hill or valley, of course. There's no doubt it looks flat. At the seaside the water seems to stretch on forever, as far as the eye can see.

But suppose on a clear day we look through a pair of binoculars at a distant ship. As it travels away from us, it seems to sink as it disappears over the horizon.

This is because the Earth is actually round. It is a ball 7,926 miles (12,756 km) across.

GOING DOWN

Right under our feet, nearly 8,000 miles (13,000 km) down, is the other side of the Earth. What keeps the people who live there from falling off?

First we have to stop thinking that there is some special direction in space called "down," such that everything is pulled in that direction. All directions in space are similar to one another. The important thing is that when something falls, it falls *toward* the Earth—it is the Earth that does the pulling.

To do this, our planet uses a force, an invisible one, called **gravity**. The strength of this force depends on how far away you are from the Earth. The bigger the distance, the weaker the force. If you go twice the distance away from the Earth's center, the force drops to a quarter; three times the distance, a ninth; ten times the distance, a hundredth; and so on. But although it gets weaker and weaker, it never completely disappears; it stretches out into space, to infinity.

★ ★ ★ ★ ★ ★ ★ ★ ★ ★

Although the Earth is round, it's not a perfect sphere—it bulges slightly at the equator. The diameter through the center of the Earth is 7,900 miles from pole to pole, but 7,926 miles across the equator. Similarly, the Earth's circumference is 24,861 miles from pole to pole, but 24,902 miles around the equator.

★ ★ ★ ★ ★ ★ ★ ★ ★ ★

The force is strongest on the surface of the Earth. Gravity is what holds you down in your seat at this very moment. If you get up and jump, gravity will pull you back again.

Now, if you and I are pulled toward the center of the Earth, the same will be true of everyone else, wherever they are on the surface of the Earth. They will all talk about being pulled "down." But all their "downs" are different.

THE FORCE THAT SHAPES THE UNIVERSE

It is not just the things outside the Earth that feel the pull of gravity; the stuff that makes up the Earth itself feels it too. Every part of the Earth is pulling on every other part of it. That's why the Earth ends up round; it's the best way of packing things together so that they can all get as close as possible to one another. All the bits of rock and dirt try to get to the center of the Earth, but they are stopped by others that got there first.

Why am I telling you this? The point is, even before we get in our rocket and leave the Earth, we already have some idea of what we are likely to find out on our travels. If the Earth attracts everything with gravity, then perhaps everything we'll come across in space attracts everything else with gravity. In fact, we shall find *it is the force of gravity that shapes the entire universe.* Not only that, but if being round is the most practical shape for the Earth, then most things out there are likely to be round too.

★ ★ ★ ★ ★ ★ ★ ★ ★ ★ ★ ★ ★ ★ ★ ★ ★ ★ ★

Gravity makes every part of the Earth pull on every other part and tries to drag them all to the center. That's why our planet is round.

★ ★ ★ ★ ★ ★ ★ ★ ★ ★ ★ ★ ★ ★ ★ ★ ★ ★ ★

"How come people on the other side of the world don't fall off?"

"How come people on the other side of the world don't fall off?"

STAYING IN SHAPE

Another thought: if we need the ground to keep gravity from pulling us straight to the center of the Earth, then other objects out in space probably have a means of supporting themselves.

Now that might seem obvious. But, strangely, some objects have great difficulty doing that; their gravity is so strong that they collapse in on themselves—with spectacular results!

I mustn't jump the gun; that will come later.

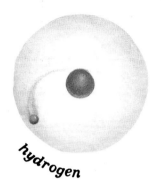

hydrogen

WHAT IS MATTER?

I've used the word "dirt" for the stuff that the Earth is made of, but "matter" is a better word. Everything is made of matter, including our own bodies.

There are hundreds of thousands of different kinds of matter in the world.

helium

What a lot to have to remember! Fortunately, there's no need. All these different kinds of matter are made up of **atoms**, and there are only 92 different kinds of atoms. So all we have to deal with are 92 kinds of building blocks—and only a few of these are important.

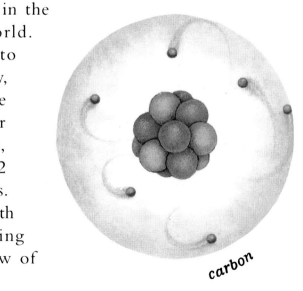

carbon

ATOMS

Each atom is made up of a small central object called the **nucleus** and, buzzing around this, even smaller particles called **electrons**. Atoms differ from one another in two ways: the size of their nucleus, and the number of electrons they have. The nucleus is made up of two types of basic particle called **protons** and **neutrons**.

A gas called **hydrogen** has the simplest atoms; a hydrogen atom has the lightest nucleus (a single proton) and only one electron. Another gas, **helium**, is next; its nucleus has two neutrons and two protons and is about four times as heavy as the nucleus of hydrogen. Outside this nucleus are two electrons. **Carbon** is an especially important atom when it comes to making the bodies of living creatures. Carbon can appear as soot, and even as diamond. Its nucleus is about 12 times as heavy as that of hydrogen, and it has six electrons. The heaviest atom is uranium, a radioactive solid. Its nucleus is about 234 times heavier than that of hydrogen, and it has 92 electrons.

One of the surprising things about an atom is that almost the whole of its insides is empty space!

Out in space, we shall be on the lookout for exactly the same kinds of atom that we are able to examine here at home. We shall be seeking answers to questions such as "Where did all of this matter come from?" and "Why is it this partic-ular mix of atoms rather than some other?"

Atoms are mostly empty space inside, which means you and I are mostly empty space too!

uranium

LOOKING UP

When we look up at the sky, to where we shall soon be heading, what do we see? The **Sun**, the Moon, and the **stars**. They are all moving slowly across the sky and around our planet. Or are they? They certainly appear to be. But people have been fooled by appearances before. Learning things often involves unlearning things first. (Remember the "down" that wasn't everyone's "down.")

For example, people used to think the sky was a great hollow dome, with twinkly lights (the stars) stuck to it. They were amazed to learn that it wasn't so. Not only that, but the stars, the Sun and the Moon were not going around the Earth once every 24 hours. It was the Earth that was spinning. The Earth completes one of its turns every 24-hour day.

When people still believed everything went around the Earth, we thought we were at the center of the universe. That meant we human beings must be very important. We *are* important (at least, I think so), but not for that reason. This is an example of the way discoveries about the universe can raise interesting questions about ourselves.

The fact that the Earth spins like a top leads us to

expect that most other things we shall discover
in our travels will also be spinning.

WHERE TO?

The largest objects in the sky are, of course, the Sun and
Moon. They appear to be roughly the same size. But again
we must be careful. The apparent size of something depends
on how far away it is.

In fact, the Moon is much closer. It is our nearest
neighbor in space. So it sounds like a good place, at long
last, to start our space journey.

★ ★ ★ ★ ★ ★ ★ ★ ★

*The Moon is almost 400
times closer to the Earth
than the Sun is, and 100
times closer than the
nearest planet.*

★ ★ ★ ★ ★ ★ ★ ★ ★

Quiz

1. Name three ways in which people have been
fooled by appearances, and later had to change
their ideas about the world.

2. How far would you have to travel from the
Earth before its gravity became zero?

3. Someone tells you the only difference between
an atom of hydrogen and an atom of carbon is that
they have a different number of electrons. What
would you say to set them straight?

Answers on page 86

FIRST STOP THE MOON

Three... two... one... blast off!

As we approach the Moon, the first thing we notice is that it is a round ball; it is not a flat disk, which is what it looks like from Earth. (But a round ball is the shape we expect from gravity, right?)

Secondly, the Man in the Moon has disappeared! His face, with those staring eyes and the open mouth which always seems to be saying "Oooh," has broken up into mountains and valleys pitted with deep holes and craters. These were made by **meteoroids**, thousands of rocks that fly through space and crash into anything that gets in their way.

Unlike the meteoroids, we land our craft gently.

GOING FOR A STROLL

Walking on the Moon is fun. You feel very light. You can take big, big steps. And boy how you can jump! Six times as high as on the Earth.

This is because the Moon's gravity force is not as strong as the Earth's—only one sixth. Your weight depends on the gravity force. If gravity is only one-sixth as strong, your weight on the Moon will be only one-sixth of your weight on the Earth.

Why is the Moon's gravity so much less than the Earth's? The Moon does not have as much **mass** as the Earth; it is not as heavy. In the first place, it is smaller. In the second, the material from which it is made has a lower **density**; it is not packed together as tightly as the Earth's material.

But although the Moon's gravity is weak, notice that *it does have a gravity force.* (Don't be fooled by those pictures of astronauts floating around weightless inside their spacecraft.) Remember, *everything* has a gravity force.

GIVE ME AIR!

Because the Moon's gravity is so weak, there is no **atmosphere** here; the Moon can't hold on to one. The atmosphere, if there ever was one, just floated away. There is no air, no water, no life—all very different from the Earth.

This is why astronauts must wear space suits on the Moon; they have to carry their own supply of air to breathe.

★ ★ ★ ★ ★ ★ ★ ★ ★

The Moon's diameter is 2,160 mi. (3,476 km). That is roughly equal to the distance across Australia. It would take 81 Moons to weigh the same as Earth.

★ ★ ★ ★ ★ ★ ★ ★ ★

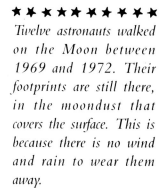

★ ★ ★ ★ ★ ★ ★ ★ ★

Twelve astronauts walked on the Moon between 1969 and 1972. Their footprints are still there, in the moondust that covers the surface. This is because there is no wind and rain to wear them away.

★ ★ ★ ★ ★ ★ ★ ★ ★

★ ★ ★ ★ ★ ★ ★ ★ ★

Will the Moon fall out of the sky?

★ ★ ★ ★ ★ ★ ★ ★ ★

★ ★ ★ ★ ★ ★ ★ ★ ★

The Moon is winning its tug of war with the Earth. It is slowly moving away from the Earth by about 2 in (3 cm) a year.

THINGS THAT GO BUMP IN THE NIGHT

And talking about gravity, here is something else for us to think about.

We traveled about 238,600 miles (384,000 km) to get here from Earth. A long way, but it is still not infinity. From what we have already learned about gravity, we know that the Earth's gravity stretches this far. The Earth is actually pulling on the Moon; it is trying to pull the Moon toward itself. Does that mean the Moon is going to fall out of the sky one night and land on our heads?

THE MERRY-GO-ROUND

No. The Moon is going around and around the Earth in an almost circular path called an **orbit**. Left to themselves, things usually move in straight lines. To get them to do anything else, like go around in a circle, you have to pull on them sideways. Remember what it is like to ride on a merry-go-round in the park? You have to hold on tight to the rail. It pulls you with a force aimed at the center of the merry-go-round. But that does not mean you end up at the center. You need that force just to stay at the same distance from the center as you go around. If you let go, you would go flying off in a straight line.

KEEPING YOUR DISTANCE

The same thing happens with the Moon. It is trying to go past the Earth in a straight line. But the sideways pull of the Earth's gravity makes its path curve, in an orbit. It's all gravity can do to keep the Moon from flying off in to space in a straight line; there's no force left over to pull it any closer to the Earth's surface.

This idea is important: if something is pulling on you with a gravity force, you don't have to crash into it. Instead, you can cancel out its gravity by going into an orbit around it. Clever, don't you think? We will come across this sort of thing again and again in our tour of the universe.

THE FAR SIDE

Just as the Earth spins around like a top as it orbits the Sun, so the Moon spins too. It takes 27.3 days, roughly one month, to spin around once, which is the same time it takes to orbit the Earth. And that means we always see the same side of the Moon on Earth. We call this side the near side. Until a spacecraft sent back photographs in 1959, no one had ever seen the far side. What did the photos show? Oddly, many many more craters than on the near side.

And now we must leave the Moon. "Already?" you ask. I'm afraid so. Quite frankly, our travels have much more exciting things in store!

Quiz

1. You weigh less on the Moon. Does that mean space travel helps to keep you slim?

2. The Earth's gravity pulls on the Moon. Does the Moon's gravity affect the Earth? Or is it too weak to reach that far?

Answers on page 86

★ ✷ ★ ✷ ★ ✷ ★ ✷ ★

More than one million Earths could fit inside the Sun.

★ ✷ ★ ✷ ★

THE SUN

A  THAT GOES OFF S L O W L Y

As seen from the Earth, the Moon and the Sun may look similar. In fact, they are very different. The Moon is a round dusty rock; the Sun is a huge ball of flaming hot gas. And I do mean huge; the distance from one side of the Sun to the other, its diameter, is 870,000 miles (1.4 million km). That is 109 times the diameter of the Earth. The reason it doesn't look a lot bigger than the Moon is that the Sun is much farther away.

Because the Sun's gas is so hot, it swirls and rushes and jiggles around a lot. You might think that all this movement would throw the gas off into space. But no. The Sun has 333,000 times the mass of the Earth, and it has an *enormous* gravity force. It is this force that keeps the gas together.

NEXT STOP THE SUN?

So, with all this gravity, is the Earth being pulled ever closer to the Sun? Happily no, as I'm sure you've already guessed. And this is for the same reason that the Moon does not fall to the Earth. Just as the Moon orbits the Earth, so the Earth orbits the Sun. It does this once every 365 days—in other words, once a year. And it stays at a distance of roughly 93 million miles (150 million km) from the Sun. That is a long way. A spacecraft traveling at the speed of a jumbo jet would take about 20 years to get to the Sun. (That's a lot of in-flight movies!) If, like an airplane flight, the fare was based on a rate of about 18 cents per mile, a return ticket would cost nearly $1.7 billion!

★ ✷ ★ ✷ ★ ✷ ★ ✷ ★

take-off . . .

★ ✷ ★ ✷ ★ ✷ ★ ✷ ★

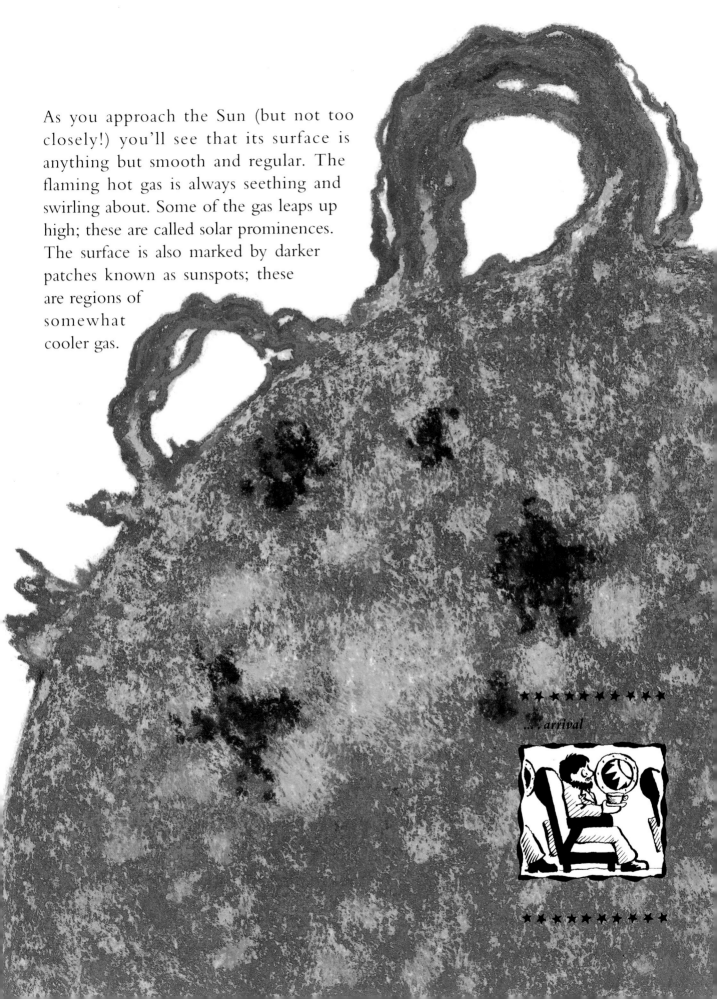

As you approach the Sun (but not too closely!) you'll see that its surface is anything but smooth and regular. The flaming hot gas is always seething and swirling about. Some of the gas leaps up high; these are called solar prominences. The surface is also marked by darker patches known as sunspots; these are regions of somewhat cooler gas.

...arrival

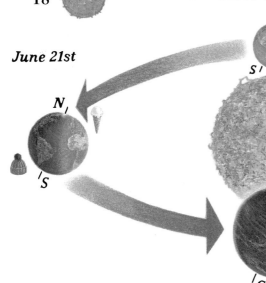

June 21st

December 21st

SPRING, SUMMER, FALL, WINTER

The Earth's orbit around the Sun is almost a circle, but not quite. It is slightly squashed. We call its oval shape an ellipse. So our distance from the Sun varies slightly during the year it takes us to complete the orbit. Is this why we have hot weather in summer and cold in winter?

No. The effect of this varying distance is very tiny. The real reason for the different seasons has to do with the way the Earth spins while it is orbiting the Sun. As we have already learned, the Earth spins like a top. It does this around an imaginary line that joins the North and South poles and is called the axis.

winter

summer

Looking at the diagram, you can see how this North-South axis is tilted to one side. Suppose it was *not* like this. Suppose it was bolt upright. Then there would be no seasons; the weather would stay the same all year round. The only effect of spinning would be to give us night and day— night when we were facing away from the Sun, day when we faced toward it.

But that is not how the axis is arranged. It is tilted. So, if we live in the North, at one stage of the orbit the axis tends to tip us slightly toward the Sun—the Sun beats down on us and we get long, hot summer days. Meanwhile, those living in the South are pointed away from the Sun; its rays hit them at only a glancing angle, and that's when they get their winter. On the opposite side of the orbit, six months later, we change places; it is then our turn to have winter, and theirs to have summer.

★ ★ ★ ★ ★ ★ ★ ★ ★

Sunlight takes 8.3 minutes to reach Earth. That means the Sun you see now is actually how the Sun looked 8.3 minutes ago.

★ ★ ★ ★ ★ ★ ★ ★ ★

PHEW! IT'S HOT!

It's a good thing we stay a long way from the Sun. The temperature of its surface is about 10,000°F (6,000°C).

And that is just the temperature of the surface. Deep down inside the Sun, the temperature increases. It becomes hotter and hotter, until right at the very center of the Sun the temperature is 27 million°F (15 million°C).

★ ★ ★ ★ ★ ★ ★ ★ ★

The temperature of ice is 32°F (0°C) and boiling water is 212°F (100°C). Think about how hot 10,000°F (6,000°C) must be!

THE SUN'S CENTRAL HEATING SYSTEM

The Sun pours out heat and light all the time. How does it manage to do this and still stay hot? What kind of fuel does it use to keep its fires burning? The answer is **nuclear fuel**—which stores the same kind of energy you get in a hydrogen bomb.

The heart of the fire is deep down in the central core of the Sun. It has been burning for 4.6 billion years. When you stop to think about it, that is really quite amazing. A hydrogen bomb going off *slowly*!

There are times when it appears as if the Sun's great fire has gone out. This is when the Moon passes between us and the Sun and blocks our view of the Sun. We call this an eclipse. When will the Sun's fire *really* go out? The Sun has enough fuel to last another 5 billion years.

FUEL FOR FIRES

What exactly is this nuclear fuel that the Sun burns? Well, first we need to look at a more familiar source of energy.

We already know that everything around us is made up of atoms—different arrangements of 92 kinds of atoms. We can change one kind of stuff into another by changing the arrangement of its atoms.

In some cases atoms give out energy as they change around—energy they no longer need with their new arrangement. That is what happens when normal fuels (things like paper, wood, and coal) change into ash and gases. They give out energy (heat and light) as they burn.

The same kind of thing can happen with the nuclei at the center of atoms. They too can sometimes join up, or split apart, to make different nuclei. And in some of these cases, energy is again given out—**nuclear energy**.

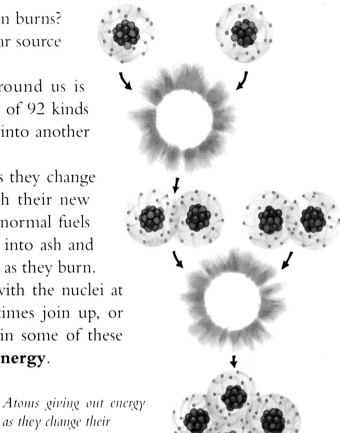

Atoms giving out energy as they change their arrangement.

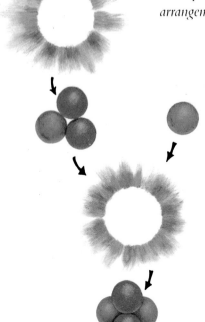

Nuclei giving out energy as they change their arrangement.

In the Sun, and in hydrogen bombs, the nuclei of hydrogen (the lightest atom) fuse together, forming the nuclei of helium (the next lightest atom). In doing so, they give out energy—a lot of energy, much more than you get when fusing atoms.

To get a fire going, you need to raise the temperature. In the case of a bonfire, this is done by first lighting a match. For the fusion of hydrogen nuclei, you need the kind of temperature you get only in places like the middle of the Sun. Only then can the **nuclear fusion** begin and the nuclear energy come pouring out—as heat and light.

OUR FRIENDLY SUN

"Huge," "flaming hot," "nuclear bomb;" that is how we have described the Sun. It doesn't sound very friendly, does it!

And yet without the Sun there would be no life on Earth. It is the Sun's rays that keep the Earth warm. Not only that, they make plants grow; they provide the energy needed to rearrange the atoms of dirt, air, and water into the stuff of leaves and branches. The atoms are rearranged a second time when the plants are eaten by animals. This time, some of the Sun's energy is released. That's how animals get the energy they need in order to grow and move about and do things. More of the energy is released when we humans eat plants and the meat of animals. That's how we get the energy we need to live.

But notice where all this energy came from in the first place—the Sun.

Quiz

1. How is the Earth's axis positioned during spring and fall?

2. Can you guess why it might be so difficult for scientists to arrange for a hydrogen bomb to go off slowly and peacefully in a laboratory? (Clue: think about the temperature needed.)

3. You weigh only one-sixth of your normal weight on the Moon. If you weighed yourself on the Sun, would you expect to be heavier or lighter than normal?

Answers on page 86

VISITING THE NEIGHBORS

The Earth is not the only planet going around the Sun. There are eight others. And what a mixed bunch they are!

THE PLANETS NEXT DOOR

We start with Mercury, the planet closest to the Sun. It races around the Sun at 30 miles (48 km) per second, completing its orbit in only 88 days instead of the Earth's sluggardly 365. Like all the planets, Mercury is also spinning on its axis. It spins more slowly than the Earth, taking 59 days for a full turn instead of one. This makes it look as if the Sun is passing across the sky incredibly slowly. So much so that Mercury's "day" (from noon one day to noon the next) is twice as long as its "year" (one orbit around the Sun). That means you would get two birthdays every day!

But before you rush to set up house on Mercury, think about this: because Mercury is so much closer to the Sun than the Earth is, the Sun looks almost three times as big from this planet. During the day, the temperature is 662°F (350°C); at night it drops to minus 365°F (-185°C). Mercury looks a bit like the Moon, with lots of craters, and like the Moon, it has no atmosphere. It is definitely not the sort of place where I would want to live.

★ ★ ★ ★ ★ ★ ★ ★ ★

◄ *Mercury*
Diameter: 3,032 mi.
Average distance from Sun: 36 million mi.
Speed: 30 mi./second.
Rotation: 59 days.
"Day": 176 days.
"Year": 88 days.

★ ★ ★ ★ ★ ★ ★ ★ ★

★ ★ ★ ★ ★ ★ ★ ★ ★ ★

▼ *Venus*
Diameter: 7,521 mi.
Average distance from
Sun: 67 million mi.
Speed: 22 mi./second.
Rotation (backward):
243 days.
"Day": 117 days.
"Year": 225 days.

★ ★ ★ ★ ★ ★ ★ ★ ★ ★

The next planet out from the Sun is Venus. It spins very slowly, in the opposite direction to the Earth's spin.

Venus is about the same size as the Earth and does have an atmosphere. But it is not the type of atmosphere we humans need for breathing. It is mostly a gas called carbon dioxide. One of the interesting things about this gas is the way it prevents heat escaping from the planet; it acts like a thick blanket. The result? The Sun's rays get trapped, and the surface of Venus becomes extremely hot: 860°F (460°C). That is hot enough to melt lead. No other planet is that hot, not even Mercury, the closest to the Sun. But it gets worse. High above this blanket of gas, clouds full of acid rain swirl around the planet, blown along by winds of up to 224 miles (360 km) per hour.

As we continue our journey out from the Sun, we come next to the Earth. I don't have to tell you about that one!

Earth
Diameter: 7,926 mi.
Average distance from
Sun: 93 million mi.
Speed: 18.6 mi./second.
Rotation/Day: 24 hours.
Year: 365.25 days.

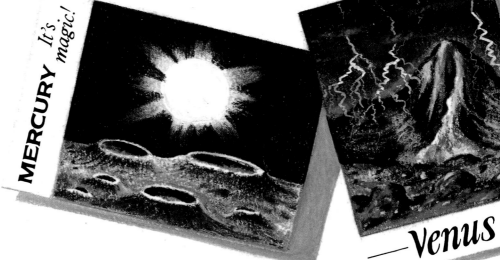

MERCURY It's magic!

Venus

Just beyond the Earth's orbit we get to Mars. People used to think that Mars might be a good place to search for life. But space probes have found none. It just seems to be a world of dead volcanoes, craters, very little atmosphere, and raging dust storms. Mars may look red-hot; in fact it's very cold, with an average temperature of minus 58°F (-50°C).

Mars has a couple of very small moons called Phobos and Deimos. These two are so small that they've never had enough gravity to pull all their matter into a tight round ball—that's why they've ended up lumpy and misshapen, like potatoes.

So much for the four rocky planets close to the Sun. Farther out we get four very different planets, all of them HUGE.

★ ★ ★ ★ ★ ★ ★ ★ ★ ★

▲ *Mars*
Diameter: 4,217 mi.
Average distance from Sun: 142 million mi.
Speed: 15 mi./second.
Rotation/"Day": 24 hours, 37 minutes.
"Year": 1.9 years.

★ ★ ★ ★ ★ ★ ★ ★ ★ ★

Mars
Wish you were here!

EARTH

Moonwalk '69

Ganymede

▲ *Jupiter*
Diameter: 88,734 mi.
Average distance from
Sun: 484 million mi.
Speed: 8 mi./second.
Rotation/"Day": 9 hours,
50 minutes.
"Year": 11.9 years.

★ ★ ★ ★ ★ ★ ★ ★ ★ ★

▶ *Saturn*
Diameter: 74,600 mi.
Average distance from
Sun: 870 million mi.
Speed: 6 mi./second.
Rotation/"Day":
10 hours, 40 minutes.
"Year": 29.5 years.

★ ★ ★ ★ ★ ★ ★ ★ ★ ★

A GIANT AMONG GIANTS

The first is Jupiter—the largest planet of all, with a diameter 11 times that of the Earth. Like the other giant planets, it is mostly a ball of hydrogen and helium. This is in the form of gas at the surface, but deeper down the gas gets packed together so thickly it becomes more like a liquid than a gas. At the center is a core of hot, molten rock, somewhat like the molten lava that comes out of volcanoes on Earth. In other words, there is probably nothing solid about Jupiter, or the other big planets. There's no ground where you can stand and say, "I'm standing on the planet, and what is above me is the planet's atmosphere." In a sense, it is all atmosphere, much like the Sun itself.

When it comes to moons, Jupiter has plenty—16! Ganymede is more than 3,100 miles (5,000 km) across; it's the biggest moon of all.

ICY RINGS, FROZEN MOONS

Next comes Saturn, second in size only to Jupiter. It is famous for being surrounded by many beautiful, wide, flat **rings**. These are not solid as you might think; they are made up of a vast number of pieces of ice. Some are the size of snowflakes, others are as big as snowballs, and the largest are several yards across. They all move around Saturn in orbit like tiny, tiny moons.

Saturn is not alone in having rings, the other three giant planets also have them. But compared to those of Saturn, they are fewer and much harder to see.

Saturn also holds the record for moons—18 of them at the last count—though some are very small. One of them, Titan, is large, larger even than planet Mercury. And it has an atmosphere twice as dense as that of Earth. So scientists wonder whether there might be some form of life on this moon. It would be a very simple form because Titan is a long way from the Sun and is very, very cold. It is like an Earth that has been kept in cold storage. We'll have to wait for some future space probe to pay it a visit before we find out whether there's any early form of life there.

Titan

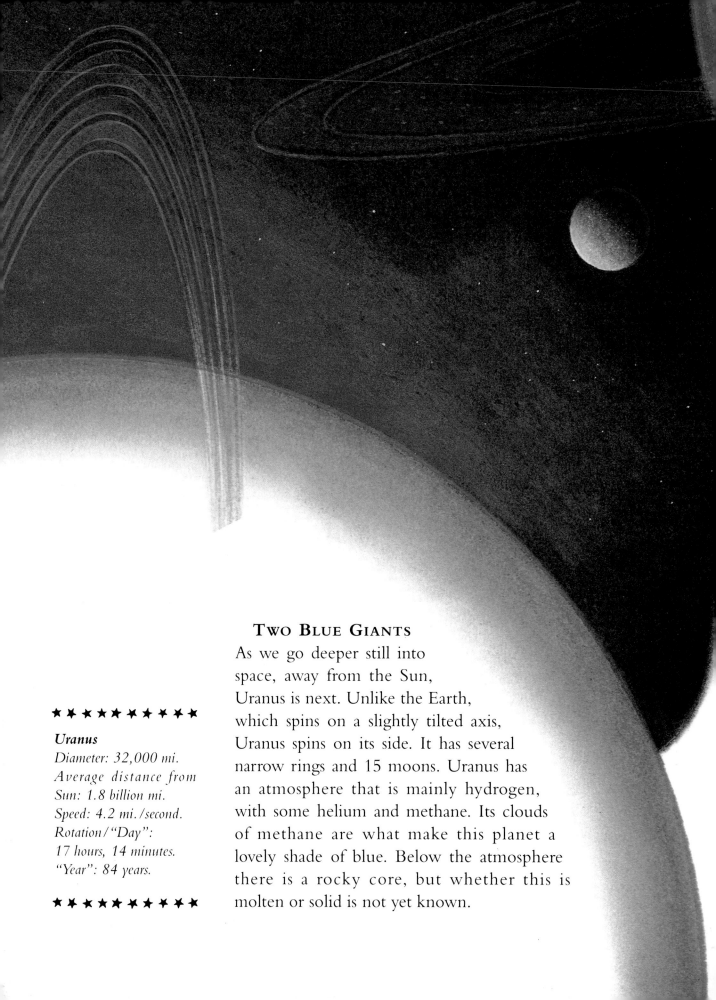

TWO BLUE GIANTS

As we go deeper still into space, away from the Sun, Uranus is next. Unlike the Earth, which spins on a slightly tilted axis, Uranus spins on its side. It has several narrow rings and 15 moons. Uranus has an atmosphere that is mainly hydrogen, with some helium and methane. Its clouds of methane are what make this planet a lovely shade of blue. Below the atmosphere there is a rocky core, but whether this is molten or solid is not yet known.

★ ★ ★ ★ ★ ★ ★ ★ ★

Uranus
Diameter: 32,000 mi.
Average distance from Sun: 1.8 billion mi.
Speed: 4.2 mi./second.
Rotation/"Day":
17 hours, 14 minutes.
"Year": 84 years.

★ ★ ★ ★ ★ ★ ★ ★ ★

Then comes Neptune, the second blue planet. Savage winds tear across this planet at 1,400 miles (2,200 km) per hour. Far above the storms, eight moons and a few rings orbit more peacefully. One of the moons, Triton, is almost as big as our own Moon. Triton is the coldest place we know—it's minus 390°F (-235°C) there.

★ ★ ★ ★ ★ ★ ★ ★ ★

Neptune
Diameter: 30,200 mi.
Average distance from Sun: 2.8 billion mi.
Speed: 3.4 mi./second.
Rotation/"Day": 18 hours, 26 minutes.
"Year": 165 years.

★ ★ ★ ★ ★ ★ ★ ★ ★

P.S. PLUTO

Lastly, beyond the giant planets there is Pluto, the smallest planet of all. A ball of rock and ice covered with nitrogen, Pluto has only one-fifth the diameter of Earth. It is so far away that it takes 248 years to complete one huge orbit around the Sun. Pluto has an elliptical orbit, long and squashed and tilted at a different angle from those of the other planets. For 20 years of its orbit Pluto actually comes closer to the Sun than Neptune; for those 20 years Neptune is the most distant planet of all. Another thing about Pluto is that, like Uranus, it spins on its side.

Pluto's moon, Charon, is large for a moon; it has half the diameter of its "parent" planet. Not only that, but it is 20 times closer to Pluto than our Moon is to Earth. Which means that Charon must look huge in the sky over Pluto—seven times bigger than our Moon does over Earth.

★ ★ ★ ★ ★ ★ ★ ★ ★

▼ *Pluto*
Diameter: 1,470 mi.
Average distance from Sun: 3.7 billion mi.
Speed: 2.9 mi./second.
Rotation/"Day": 6 days, 9 hours.
"Year": 248 years.

★ ★ ★ ★ ★ ★ ★ ★ ★

THE SUN'S FAMILY

So there we have it, the nine planets. As I said, a very mixed bunch, varying greatly in size and the stuff from which they are made. They vary in temperature, too—from the 860°F (460°C) heat of Venus to the minus 455°F (-220°C) chill on the surface of distant Neptune.

Note that only one planet has the right kind of temperature and materials to be a home for advanced forms of life: the Earth!

To complete the picture, there are the **asteroids**. These are thousands of rocks that form a band between the orbits of Mars and Jupiter. The largest is a third of the size of our Moon, the smallest are like grains of sand. Asteroids are probably the building blocks of a would-be planet that never formed.

And finally there are balls of dirty ice called **comets**. They spend most of their time in orbit around the Sun far beyond Pluto's orbit. Some of them, however, have very squashed orbits which occasionally bring them in close to the Sun. When this happens, they heat up and give off steam and gas which form a "tail" that can sometimes be seen with the naked eye from Earth.

Meteoroids are chunks of stone and iron left behind by comets and asteroids. When they rain down on our atmosphere, most of them burn up as harmless **meteors**. Some meteors are large enough to blaze right through the atmosphere as fireballs. These fireballs either explode or crash to the ground as **meteorites**.

Altogether, the Sun, the planets, moons and rings, the asteroids and comets, add up to what we call the **Solar System**. The Solar System is like a flat disk, with the Sun at the center. The planets are spread out over the disk, and they are all going around the center in the same direction as the Sun itself is spinning—counterclockwise if you look at them from above the Earth's North Pole. This is also the direction in which the Earth spins on its axis. What keeps them all going around and around? The "merry-go-round" force provided by the Sun's gravity.

Quiz

1. Which planet, Mercury or Jupiter, would you expect to have the longer year (that is, to take the longer time to go all the way around the Sun)?

2. Would you expect Jupiter's moon, Ganymede, to be hotter or colder on average than our Moon?

Answers on page 87

BIRTH OF THE SUN

How did the Solar System get the way it is? How did it form? We cannot be sure of the details, but most scientists think the story goes something like this....

THE BIG SQUEEZE

Deep in space there are clouds of gas, dust, and ice crystals. Long ago, there was just such a cloud. It was more or less round and turned slowly on its axis—much like the Earth spins on its north-south axis. But then the cloud began to collapse in on itself. The outer particles were pulled inward by the gravity forces of the particles nearer the center.

The particles near the "poles" fell quickly, those being whirled around near the "equator" not so quickly—because some of the gravity there was being used up to provide the "merry-go-round" force. In this way the cloud became flattened. Lots of material squashed together at the center; the rest was spread out in the shape of a disk at the equator.

As the particles fell, they speeded up. When they crashed together at the center, all the energy from these collisions heated up the gas. It became so hot that when hydrogen nuclei collided they could now fuse together and release bursts of nuclear energy. That was how the nuclear fire got started. And once started, it continued burning. The Sun had been born.

PILES OF DIRT

Meanwhile, what was happening outside the Sun?

In the slowly rotating disk, grains of dust and ice moved around, bumping into each other. Sometimes they stuck together to make a larger grain. This larger grain, because of its size, had an even better chance of bumping into another grain and getting stuck to that, too. In this way, certain grains got bigger and bigger. They became rocks and lumps of ice. Still they grew. Now they had a gravity force strong enough to pull other pieces of rock and ice toward them. A few became so big they swept up almost all the others. In the end there were nine huge round balls—the nine planets!

For a long time after the planets had formed, they continued to be hit by smaller rocks flying around. These rocks, called meteorites, caused the craters on the Moon and Mercury. They caused craters on the Earth too, but not many are left; most have been worn away by wind and rain.

Some scientists think that, 65 million years ago, a particularly large meteorite crashed into the Earth. Clouds of debris blocked out the sunlight, temperatures dropped and many forms of life, including the dinosaurs, were wiped out.

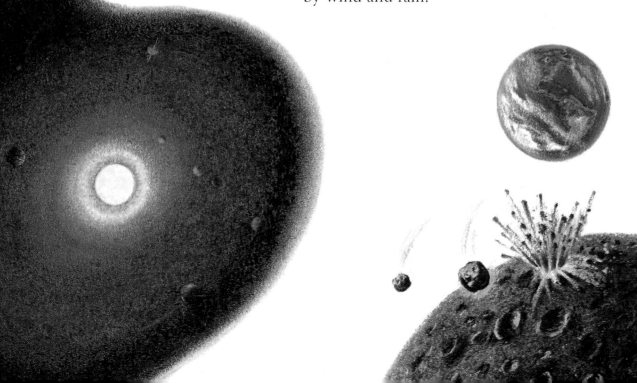

NEW MOONS

Just as the planets
formed out of the dusty disk that
surrounded the Sun's equator, so moons
formed out of dusty disks surrounding the equators
of the planets.

But not all the moons formed in this way. Some of the rocks flying through space, instead of crashing onto a planet, got captured into an orbit around it. That is how Mars probably got its two moons. Some people think our own Moon was formed from material knocked out of the Earth when it was hit by a particularly large flying rock.

As for the rings that encircle the giant planets, scientists think that these were formed out of bits of small moons that got hit and broke up.

BLOWING AWAY THE CLOUDS

Like the Sun itself, most of the disk outside the Sun was made of the lightest gases—hydrogen and helium. What became of them?

The gases were captured by the gravity of each of the newly forming planets and formed their atmospheres. Once the Sun caught fire though, the hydrogen and helium belonging to the four nearest planets got very hot—so hot that some of the fast-moving particles of these gases could now escape the pull of the planet's gravity, and others were blown away by a strong wind coming from the Sun. Mercury, being the closest to the Sun, and not having a very strong gravity, lost all its atmosphere. Venus, Earth, and Mars were left with only heavier gases, such as carbon dioxide and nitrogen. Later, once life had developed, oxygen was added to the Earth's atmosphere. That's because plants take in carbon dioxide and give out oxygen in exchange.

THE SUN THAT
DID NOT MAKE IT

Far away from the Sun,
the hydrogen and helium
collected around the four
giant planets. These planets
are so cold, and their gravity
so strong, that they are able to hold
on to even the lightest gases. In fact,
the giant planets are mostly made of these
two gases.

The largest of the planets, Jupiter, almost became
a second sun. As its gases squashed down to become a tight
ball, they heated up, just as the gases did in the Sun. Even
today, the temperature at the center of Jupiter is over
36,000°F (20,000°C). The rise in temperature, however, was
never enough to trigger a nuclear fire. The hydrogen nuclei
banged into each other all right, but not hard enough to
fuse; so no extra nuclear energy was given out. The
result? This would-be sun just fizzled out.

Why did the temperature not get higher?
Jupiter is smaller than the Sun, and its gravity
is weaker. When it pulled in new
particles, it could not make them go
fast enough. To do that, Jupiter
would have had to be 70 times
heavier than it is.

AND THE PLANET THAT NEVER MADE IT

Jupiter might have been too small to be a sun, but as a planet it was big. Its gravity force was so strong that it kept upsetting the paths of nearby rocks. As a result, these were never able to settle down to form a planet of their own. That is why there are asteroids in the gap between Mars and Jupiter instead of another planet.

Jupiter has captured some of the asteroids as extra moons. Others it has thrown so far off course that they crash onto other planets. Scientists are very interested in collecting any such rocks falling on the Earth. They are leftovers from the early Solar System. By studying them, scientists can learn what the first rocks were like before they came together to form the planets. These clues help build up a history of the Solar System.

Jupiter sends an asteroid out of the ballpark.

Quiz

1. Why do we see so many more craters on the Moon and on Mercury than we do on the Earth?

2. In the last chapter we saw how all the planets go around the Sun in the same direction as the Sun spins. Can you now explain this?

Answers on page 87

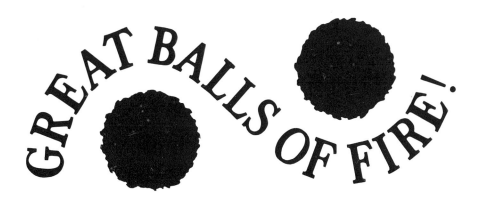

GREAT BALLS OF FIRE!

It is time to say good-bye to the Solar System. We head out to the stars. And what a long journey that turns out to be!

GETTING A CLOSE-UP VIEW

Suppose we were able to travel as fast as a light beam, 186,000 miles (300,000 km) per second. At that speed it would take eight-and-a-half minutes to reach the Sun. But to get to the nearest star, which is called Proxima Centauri, would take just over four years.

And what a surprise awaits us when we get to that star! As we approach closer and closer, the tiny point of light gets bigger and bigger. It grows into a great ball of fire. It looks just like the Sun. In fact, every star is a "sun." Or, putting it the other way around, the Sun is our very own star.

DRAWINGS IN THE SKY

For thousands of years, people have thought of the stars as being grouped together to form pictures in the sky, much like dot-to-dot drawings. These pictures are called **constellations**. I'm not very good at recognizing constellations. I can manage the Big Dipper and two or three others, but that's about it! Some people think these patterns influence our lives. They claim to be able to tell our fortunes by looking at the stars.

As we journey through space, however, we find that the stars that make up some constellations are *not* particularly

the Water Snake

the Big Dipper

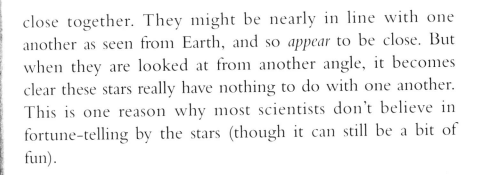

close together. They might be nearly in line with one another as seen from Earth, and so *appear* to be close. But when they are looked at from another angle, it becomes clear these stars really have nothing to do with one another. This is one reason why most scientists don't believe in fortune-telling by the stars (though it can still be a bit of fun).

DWARFS AND GIANTS

As we visit various stars we see they're not all the same. Some are yellow like the Sun, others glow with a dazzling bluish color, others with a dull red. Some are much larger than the Sun and are called **giant stars**. Others are smaller and are called **dwarf stars**. Why these differences?

A lot depends on how massive a star is, how much gas came together to form it in the first place. The Sun is a medium-sized star. If the amount of gas that formed a star was much less than that which formed the Sun, the star would not get as hot and glow as brightly; it would be a **red dwarf**. With even less gas, the temperature rise caused by the gas squashing together is not enough even to trigger a nuclear fire, and we get a **brown dwarf**. Brown dwarfs are not true stars.

The other main reason why stars look different has to do with their age, which is the topic of the next chapter.

Quiz

1. How would you explain to someone why the stars in the sky look so tiny?

2. From what you've learned in this chapter about different types of stars, how would you now describe Jupiter?

Answers on page 87

THE LIFE AND DEATH OF A STAR

Walking down a street, you are likely to see children, middle-aged people, and old people. It is the same with the stars; they all have different ages. Some have just been born, others are halfway through their active lives, and yet others are about to retire.

A PIECE OF DETECTIVE WORK

The average star lives for thousands of millions of years. So there is not much point in hanging around hoping to see how it grows old. Luckily we don't have to. On our tour around the stars just now, we saw stars at different stages of their lives. Each provides us with a "snapshot" of what a star is like at that particular age. If we put the snapshots in their proper order—starting with young stars and going on to the older ones—we can piece together what the complete life story of a single star might be.

GETTING GOING

Let's begin with a medium-sized star like the Sun. We already know how it formed out of a cloud of gas. The cloud shrank and heated up at its center, and its nuclear fire was triggered. The new star was born.

★ ✦ ★ ✦ ★ ✦ ★

Snapshots of a star

★ ✦ ★ ✦ ★ ✦ ★

KEEPING IN SHAPE

If the first problem of being a star is how to trigger your nuclear fire, the next one is how to keep your shape. A star is very heavy. So what keeps all that matter from collapsing down to a point?

Matter near the center is extremely hot. That means it is jiggling about with lots of energy. Gravity tries to pull the outer layers in toward the center, but as they get close, the jiggling particles already there knock them back up again. In this way a balance is struck: gravity pulling inward versus the jiggling motion pushing outward. So that solves the problem of how to stop the star from collapsing.

All the hot jiggling about at the center of the star keeps the outer layers of matter from squeezing in any closer.

KEEPING IT HOT

But it brings us to yet another problem: how to keep the center hot and jiggling. The difficulty is that the star is losing energy all the time. It takes about one million years for heat produced in the fire in the center to find its way to the outside of the star, but it does manage it in the end. This energy is then lost to space as heat rays and sunlight. So, if the core of the star is to stay hot, the lost energy must be replaced; the fire must keep burning.

Luckily for us, stars are very good at this. A star like the Sun can keep burning steadily for 10 billion years.

A FUEL SHORTAGE

But this can't go on forever. The nuclear fire depends on hydrogen fusing together to form helium. In time, all the hydrogen fuel at the center of the star gets used up. All that is left is helium "ash." So, in this region of the star, the nuclear fire goes out. Only in a thin shell around the outside of the dead core does the burning still go on.

What happens next? Without its fire to provide energy, the core cannot hold itself up against gravity. It starts to squash down. As it does so, it heats up (in the same way as the original gas that formed the star heated up when it squashed down). When the core reaches one fiftieth of its original size, it has become so hot that a new type of nuclear fire is triggered: helium nuclei fusing to make carbon nuclei. This is followed by some of the carbon fusing with helium to give oxygen. In this way, the star is able to squeeze a little extra nuclear energy out of the helium ash, and so hold itself up for a bit longer.

But this cannot last. In the end, all the fuel is used up. The fire goes out, and the core continues to squeeze down.

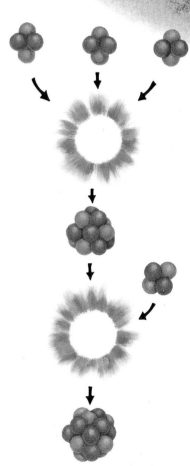

Three helium nuclei can fuse to form one nucleus of carbon. The carbon nucleus can then fuse with a helium nucleus to form oxygen.

★ ★ ★ ★ ★ ★ ★ ★ ★

MIDDLE-AGE SPREAD

Now you might think that, while all this was going on, the star would get smaller and smaller. But it doesn't! What we have been talking about is the core of the star. What about the rest of the star, its outer parts? Strange to say, while the core shrinks, the outer parts of the star swell up. Just as some people get fatter as they get older, the star develops a "middle-age spread."

When the Sun reaches this stage it may well grow to such a size that it will swallow up the Earth. (Don't worry. This is not expected to happen for another billion years!)

At this point in its life, the star has become a giant star. Because the outer parts cool down as they swell up, the light they give out changes from the yellowy-white of normal sunlight to red. For this reason the star is called a **red giant**.

The star spends about one tenth of its life as a red giant. After that, it loses its outer layer, which goes drifting off into space as a glowing cloud of gas. All that is left behind is its inner core. For the first time we are able to see this core. It is small and hot and shines with a brilliant white light. We call it a **white dwarf**.

GRAVEYARD OF THE STARS

What happens to the core in the end? As it shrinks down, the atoms become so squashed together that they are no longer separate atoms. Instead of each nucleus having its own electrons, the electrons form a kind of "soup" in which they are shared equally among all the nuclei. This soup is a very good way of packing matter together. It is very dense, which means it weighs a lot even when there isn't much of it. And it can stand enormous pressures.

And that really is that. We end up with a very hard, tightly-packed ball of electron "soup," mixed with carbon and oxygen nuclei. It is about the size of the Earth. It starts off white-hot but gradually cools down to become a cold, dead cinder. One day that will be the end of our Sun.

Quiz

1. At what phase is the Sun in its active life? Has it just begun, or is it halfway through, or is it nearly at the end?

2. Some cartoons on page 39 show a star at different stages of its life. Which picture would you say goes with each of the following four descriptions of a star? **a)** a white dwarf; **b)** a collapsing cloud of gas; **c)** a star burning hydrogen at its core; and **d)** a star where carbon and helium nuclei are fusing to form oxygen.

Answers on page 87

★ ★ ★ ★ ★ ★ ★ ★

One teaspoon of electron soup would weigh the same as 100 cars!

★ ★ ★ ★ ★ ★ ★ ★

SUPER-DENSE CINDERS

Stars can range anywhere between one twentieth and about 50 to 100 times as massive as the Sun. They don't come smaller because, as we have seen, anything less and you can't get the nuclear fire going. They also don't come larger. This is because the more massive the star, the brighter it burns. Any star trying to be much more than 100 times as massive as the Sun would give out so much light that the light itself would blast the extra matter away.

So far we have followed the life history of only those stars that are like our Sun. What about the others? In particular, what about stars that are heavier than the Sun?

BLUE GIANTS

Like the Sun, **blue giants** burn steadily for most of their lives. Being heavier, they have more matter in them, more fuel. Does that mean they burn for a longer time? No. They burn so strongly that they get through their fuel more quickly than the Sun does. A star 25 times as massive as the Sun reaches the giant stage of its life after only six million years, compared to the Sun's 10 billion years.

Because the star is hotter, it shines with a bluish-white light. For this reason we call it a blue giant.

As the outer layers swell up, what happens to the core? It goes through the same changes as the core of a star like the Sun. Except that it doesn't stop with producing carbon and oxygen. The temperature gets so high that even bigger nuclei can be fused, all the way up to the nuclei of iron. At that point, the very last bit of nuclear energy has been wrung out of the core material.

A NEUTRON CORE

Now the nuclear fire in the core goes out. The core shrinks down under the force of its own gravity. After a while, it gets to the point at which the other stars stopped shrinking, when the atoms were jam-packed together so as to form an electron soup. But this time, if the core is more than about one and a half times as massive as the Sun, the shrinking does not stop. The gravity is so strong that even the electron soup is unable to hold up the great weight lying on top of it. The electrons get pushed closer and closer toward the nuclei. Some get pushed *into* the nuclei.

This allows the matter to pack even more tightly, which means gravity is even stronger.

What happens to the electrons inside the nuclei? Nuclei are made up of two types of particles: protons and neutrons. The electrons join up with the protons to produce extra neutrons. In the end, all the electrons and protons have gone, and we are left with only neutrons. These now form one huge nucleus about 12 miles 20 km) across—"neutron soup." Neutron soup is very stiff, much stiffer than electron soup. So stiff that it prevents any more shrinking.

The new neutron core is an amazing object—to think that a massive star over 600,000 miles (1 million km) across has shrunk to this "tiny" size. And its material is amazingly dense. One teaspoonful of the stuff would weigh a billion tons, 10,000 melted-down aircraft carriers.

neutron soup

★ ★ ★ ★ ★ ★ ★ ★ ★

In the first 10 seconds, a supernova explosion produces 100 times more energy than the Sun will produce in the whole of its 10 billion year lifetime.

★ ★ ★ ★ ★ ★ ★ ★ ★

AN EXPLOSION

So much for the core of the star. What about the star's outer parts? With the inner parts collapsed, there is nothing now to hold up the outer parts. So they too start to fall. They rush toward the center. What then? Some scientists think they hit the core and bounce back. Others say they are knocked back by a flood of particles coming the other way. These particles are called **neutrinos** (not to be confused with neutrons). They come from the core. Every time an electron gets swallowed up by a proton to produce a neutron, a neutrino is also thrown out. Not only that, but the intense heat of the core produces even more neutrinos. This hail of neutrino "gunfire" blasts some of the outer parts of the star away. The result? A tremendous explosion—a **supernova**!

NEUTRINOS

Neutrinos are ghostly! At this very moment, 15 trillion neutrinos are passing through your head every second, and you don't feel a thing! These neutrinos come from nuclear processes taking place in the Sun. They are so slippery that they hardly affect anything. They easily pass through the Earth.

And yet, although they are so slippery, we believe it is mainly neutrinos that blast the material out of supernovae. They can do this because there are so many of them.

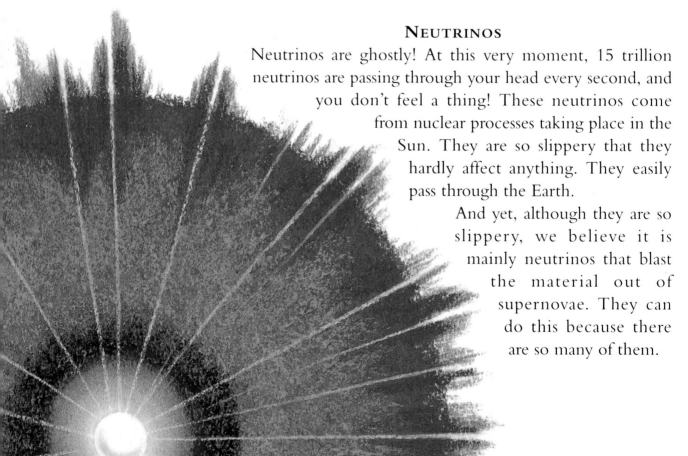

SUPERNOVAE

Supernovae explosions are the most spectacular events that ever happen in the universe. There is a blinding flash of light, so bright that for a few days this one exploding star gives out as much light as 100 billion ordinary stars. If you are lucky enough to see one of these explosions it looks as though a new star has been born. That is why they are called supernovae, meaning huge "new stars." Which is not a very good name as a supernova is not a new star at all; it is the end of an old star. Besides, the light doesn't last all that long; it soon dies down.

Supernovae don't happen that often. If you had 100 billion stars, you would still have to wait about 25 years for one of them to explode. The last one seen with the naked eye from Earth happened in 1987. But even then you could see it only if you lived in the Southern Hemisphere. I regret never having had the chance to see a supernova. Perhaps you will be luckier!

To sum up so far: a massive star collapses, a hard neutron core is formed, and the outer layers are blasted away by the burst of neutrinos given out from the core. What we are left with is a tiny hot core, now called a **neutron star**. How long does all this take? A few seconds! That's all, just a few seconds. I don't know about you, but I find that amazing. To think that the star has lived for millions of years and then, suddenly, without warning, it's all over in a matter of seconds.

This is the famous Crab Nebula where a massive supernova explosion was recorded by Chinese astronomers on July 4th, 1054. Today we can see the clouds of material still flying outward because of that great explosion. At the very center, close to where the original star used to be, a neutron star has been left behind.

★ ★ ★ ★ ★ ★ ★ ★ ★ ★

IN A SPIN

You might think that, once the neutron star has been formed, it just sits there quietly doing nothing. But that is not the case. It is spinning like crazy!

"Can you spin as fast as a neutron star?"

Remember how we have discovered that just about everything in the universe spins— the Earth, the Moon, the planets, the Sun. The same is true of big massive stars before they collapse. When something spins, we say it has **angular momentum**. How much it has depends on how heavy it is, what shape and size it has, and how fast it is spinning.

When a star collapses to a neutron core, it becomes smaller. In order to have the same angular momentum as before, it has to make up for its smaller size by speeding up. (It is the same for an ice skater. She starts by holding out her arms wide and spinning slowly. As she draws her arms in toward her body, she spins faster and faster. How she doesn't get dizzy I'll never know.)

Some neutron stars complete hundreds of turns every second. What a thought—a massively heavy ball, a couple of miles across, spinning that fast!

MIGHTY MAGNETS

There is something else I must tell you about neutron stars: they behave like very powerful magnets. You know how the Earth has magnetism; that's what makes a compass needle point north. Well, stars also have magnetism.

When a star collapses down to the size of a neutron star, its magnetism becomes concentrated. It becomes almost a trillion times stronger than the magnetism of the Earth. So we have a powerful magnet being whirled around by the neutron star's spin.

One result is that two invisible beams of radio waves are given out, one from the neutron star's north pole and one from its south pole. These beams don't always lie along the star's spin axis, so they get swung around and around, like beams from a lighthouse. If we on Earth happen to be in line with one of these beams, we pick up a pulse of radio waves every time the beam points in our direction.

That's how neutron stars were discovered. The first one showed up as a radio signal that kept repeating itself about once a second. To begin with, scientists had no idea what it could be. They even wondered whether there might be aliens out there trying to signal to us! It was called a **pulsar**, a pulsing radio source. Later, scientists realized that the source was a neutron star.

As we have seen, neutron stars must be at least one and a half times as heavy as the Sun.

When pulsars were first discovered, people thought that someone might be trying to get in touch with us. The early pulsars were called LGM 1, LGM 2 and so on; "LGM" stood for "Little Green Men"!

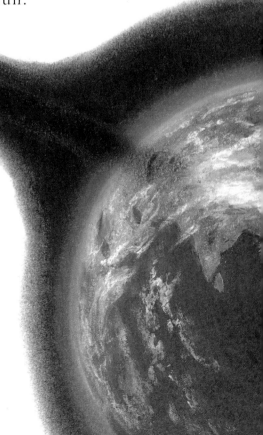

Anything lighter, and its gravity would not have been strong enough to squash the core down. That is not to say that the original star was one and a half times as heavy. It would have started out something like eight times as heavy, if not more. As a blue giant, it lost some of its material into space, and more still was blown away in the supernova explosion. So what is left is only a fraction of what there was at the beginning.

So, the neutron star cannot be lighter than one and a half times the mass of the Sun. But it must also not be too heavy. If it is two and a half times as heavy as the Sun, it is in deep trouble.

What Happens To Very Heavy Stars?

Remember how the collapse into a neutron core began when the electron soup started to buckle under the pressure; the core squashed down to a stiffer neutron soup instead. Now the same thing happens again. The gravity of the core is so enormous, even the tough inner layers of the neutron soup cannot hold up the outer ones. They too buckle and collapse in on themselves. The more tightly packed they become, the more concentrated and powerful the gravity, making it even more difficult to resist. What can resist it? Nothing! The collapse continues until all the material of the star is squashed down to a point, a point smaller than that of the thinnest, finest needle! We have now arrived at what must be the most frightening object in the universe: a **black hole**.

Black Holes

Black holes are strange. Their gravity is so power-ful that, within a certain distance of the squashed-down point, nothing, absolutely nothing, can drag itself away. Not even light itself. That's why the holes are black. In the case of a collapsed star, two and a half times as massive as the Sun, this distance would be about 4.7 miles (7.5 km). It is called the **horizon** of the black hole.

As time goes by, more and more matter passes through this horizon and gets sucked into the black hole. Everything that falls in makes the hole heavier. That means its gravity is even stronger. That in turn means the hole's horizon, the point of no return, creeps farther and farther outward.

INTO THE BLACK HOLE

What would it be like to fall into a black hole? As you got closer, you would feel you were being crushed by a great weight pressing in on you from every side. Except that, if you were falling feet first, your feet would feel as though they were being pulled off the rest of your body. This is because gravity gets stronger the closer you are to the central point, where all the matter is squashed together. Your feet, being closer, would be pulled by a stronger gravity than the rest of your body. In fact, in the last moments, they would be ripped off your legs before they, and you, were finally crushed out of existence. My advice? If ever you become an astronaut, let someone else investigate black holes!

If no light comes from the black hole, how can you see it? You can't. But you know it is there by watching matter being sucked into it.

The matter heats up as it falls toward the hole. It can then radiate some of that energy away before disappearing through the horizon.

Sometimes two stars orbit each other—stars in pairs like this are called **binary stars**. If one of them collapses down to become a black hole, we can tell it is there not only from the way matter is sucked in, but also from the way the visible star continues to orbit the black hole.

So, to sum up, what is left after stars have died? There are the cold, burned-out remains of white dwarfs, the gas and dust blasted out into space by supernovae explosions, spinning neutron stars, and black holes.

Quiz

1. A cloud of gas 200 times as massive as the Sun collects together to form a star. How massive will the star be for most of its life?

2. A star spends most of its life twice as massive as the Sun. How will it end its life: as a white dwarf, a neutron star, or a black hole? (Think carefully!)

3. What kind of matter holds up the outer layers of **a)** a white dwarf, **b)** a neutron star, and **c)** a black hole?

4. The radio waves from a pulsar look as though they are being switched on and off. But are they really pulsing like that?

5. Why do you think the boundary of a black hole is called a "horizon"?

6. How could you signal home that you had fallen beyond the horizon into a black hole and needed help?

Answers on pages 87–88

ISLAND W🌀RLDS

How many stars are there? If you look up at the sky, you can count about 6,000. If it is a dark, clear night—and you are well away from the glare of street lights—you can also make out a faintly glowing band of light stretching right across the sky from one horizon to the other. This is called the **Milky Way**. What is it?

If we imagine journeying toward it, we discover it is actually made up of stars—many, many stars, normally too far away to be seen as separate points of light. In fact, in all, there are 100 billion of them! Each as big as our Sun! That's 20 stars for every man, woman, and child on Earth. How many of those stars have planets, I wonder. And how many of those planets have life?

All of these stars are gathered together in a great swirling group called the **Galaxy**. This is shaped like a flat disk. The Milky Way glowing in the sky is simply the Galaxy seen from the side, from our own position in the disk. The disk has a bulge at the center where the stars, gas, and dust are especially dense. And then, around the disk, there is a ball of thinly spread-out stars called a halo.

★ ★ ★ ★ ★ ★ ★ ★ ★

The Galaxy seen side-on, showing its disk, bulge, and halo.

*The Galaxy seen from above,
showing its spiral arms.*

★ ✦ ★ ✦ ★ ✦ ★ ✦ ★

LOOKING BACK

As we journey out of the Galaxy, and then look back at it,
from above this time, we can see better just how huge it is.
A light beam traveling at 186,000 miles per second (300,000
km/s) takes 100,000 years to cross from one side to the
other. From here we can see its spiral arms—regions where
most of the brightly shining new stars are to be found.

Our Sun is a tiny speck about two thirds of the way out
from the center of the disk.

THE GALACTIC MERRY-GO-ROUND

What keeps all these stars from piling up on top of one another under the pull of their gravity? I'm sure you can guess the answer to that one. That's right: it's another of those "merry-go-round" forces at work again. The stars don't just sit there in space; they are all on the move. Just as the Moon keeps its distance by moving in orbit around the Earth, and the Earth by orbiting the Sun, so the Sun and all the other stars orbit around the center of the Galaxy. The whole Galaxy is spinning. Mind you, it spins very slowly; the Sun takes about 200 million years to complete one turn.

HEADING FOR TROUBLE

Sometimes a star orbiting the center of the Galaxy gets too close to another star. It gets deflected by the other star's gravity. As a result, it might now find itself heading straight for the center. What happens when it arrives there?

We cannot be sure; it is difficult to see through all the dust and gas that makes up the central bulge. But most scientists think that a lot of matter—as much as you get in one million Suns—has ended up there. It now forms a huge black hole, with a horizon as big as the Sun. And with each star it greedily gobbles up, the horizon advances outward a few miles more in its search for more victims!

THERE'S MORE TO IT THAN MEETS THE EYE

If we know the radius of a star's orbit around the center of the Galaxy, and how fast it is moving, we can figure out how strong its "merry-go-round" force has to be. It has to equal the gravity force trying to pull the star to the center. Scientists expected this gravity force would simply be whatever was produced by the other stars closer to the center.

But the sums didn't add up! The "merry-go-round" force came out ten times bigger. So why doesn't the star get flung out of the Galaxy?

Types of galaxy

elliptical

spiral

barred spiral

irregular

The answer is that there must be more matter in the Galaxy than we can see—ten times more! It is the gravity of all this extra matter that must provide most of the merry-go-round force. But what kind of matter is it? No one knows for sure. It is one of the big unsolved problems. We call it **dark matter**.

GALAXIES GALORE

What lies beyond the Galaxy? More galaxies. Powerful telescopes show that each part of the sky the size of the Moon has half a million galaxies! Our Galaxy (written with a capital "G") is just one out of 100 billion. In other words, for every man, woman, and child on Earth there are not only 20 stars in our Galaxy, but also 20 galaxies out there in space! I don't know about you, but when I think that each one of them is a swirling island of about 100 billion stars, I give up! My mind can't take it in. The study of the universe on this grandest of scales is called **cosmology**. It is one of the most thrilling of all sciences.

LEARNING FROM OTHERS

Because we look at other galaxies from the outside, we can learn things about our own Galaxy from them. For example, some other galaxies looked at from above evidently have spiral arms—a clue that we ought to search for spiral arms in our own Galaxy.

Not only that, but some galaxies appear to have a black hole at their center. Scientists have figured out that some of these galactic black holes are as heavy as hundreds of millions of Suns. It is because other galaxies seem to have black holes at their centers that we think our Galaxy does too—though at present it is probably a small, young one.

In 1994, scientists discovered what may be a super black hole at the center of galaxy M87. It is the size of our Solar System, and it has already swallowed up a billion stars.

Famous galaxies

Whirlpool

Sombrero

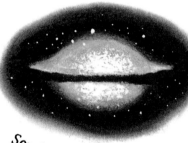

Cartwheel

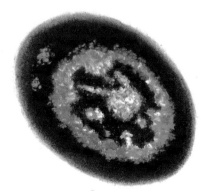

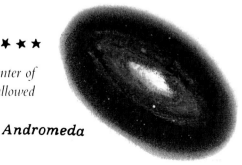

Andromeda

GALACTIC GATHERINGS

Just as stars are gathered together in galaxies, the galaxies themselves tend to stick together. Our own Galaxy is a member of a small group of about 30 galaxies called the **Local Group**. Other groups are larger, perhaps having as many as a thousand galaxies.

The groups belong to **clusters** of groups, and the clusters to superclusters. Superclusters tend to be shaped like vast walls surrounding empty spaces. You know how a sponge has holes in it. Well, the whole universe looks a bit like that—a giant galactic sponge. Why it should have such a peculiar shape is, yet again, a mystery waiting to be solved by the next generation of cosmologists.

And when I say a "giant" sponge, I mean it. The universe is colossal. Traveling at 186,000 miles (300,000 km) per second, light from the most distant galaxies yet seen has taken billions of years to reach our telescopes. Beyond them, no doubt, lie more galaxies. For all we know, the universe might reach infinitely far in all directions. In other words, it might have no boundary, no end.

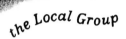

the Local Group

★ ✦ ★ ✦ ★ ✦ ★ ✦ ★

Light races through the universe at 186,000 miles per second.

★ ✦ ★ ✦ ★ ✦ ★ ✦ ★

Quiz

1. You now know of two ways in which black holes might form. What are they?

2. Someone tells you dark matter is just another name for the matter that has fallen into a black hole. Do you agree with them? If not, how would you set them straight?

3. What force do you think holds the galaxies together in groups and clusters?

Answers on page 88

THE BIG BANG

"Goodbye, galaxies."

I f gravity stretches out across space, then each galaxy will attract every other one. So, what stops them from all ending up in a pile? Are they rotating around one another to cancel out their gravity with a "merry-go-round" force?

The answer is no. The "sponge" of galaxies is not rotating. So what stops everything from collapsing together under the force of its own gravity? That is one of the mysteries about galaxies.

Distant galaxies are all going away from us. The farther away they are, the faster they are moving.

ANOTHER MYSTERY

On the very large scale, the galaxies might not be moving in orbit about one another, but they are moving. They are all moving away from us. Wherever we look in space, we see the galaxies heading off into the distance. Why are they doing that? What is so special about us that everything in the universe is trying to get away from us?

Not only that, we notice that the farther away a galaxy is, the faster it is moving. A galaxy that is three times farther away than another will be going three times as fast; ten times farther, ten times as fast; and so on. Why is that?

IN REVERSE

Suppose a film has been made of the moving galaxies. What would it look like if you ran it backward? Instead of the galaxies traveling away from us, they would now be coming toward us. When would they arrive? A galaxy three times as far away as another would have farther to go to reach us. But that doesn't mean it would arrive later. Remember: a galaxy three times farther away is traveling three times as fast. It arrives at the same time as the other. In fact, all the galaxies arrive at the same time!

Running the film backward is like running time backward. What it shows is that there must have been a time in the past when all the matter of the universe was packed tightly together.

THE BIG BANG

So, what we think happened is this: all the matter began by being squashed up. Suddenly it expanded outward, the faster matter traveling farther. That same **expansion of the universe** is going on today. That is what we see when we view the movements of the galaxies.

This great explosion is called the **Big Bang**. How long ago did it happen? We can figure it out from the speeds of the galaxies and how far they have traveled at those speeds. The answer turns out to be around 15 billion years ago.

A LONG TIME AGO

Fifteen billion years ago is so much longer than the average lifetime of a human being that it is hard to get a feeling for what it means. But if you imagine all that time reduced to just a single year, then on that scale our own lifetime would amount to about one fifth of a second!

The Big Bang explains why the galaxies are moving away from us. It also explains our first mystery: why everything does not pile up on top of one another. Although gravity does indeed try to pull everything together, the violence of that explosion is still throwing everything farther and farther apart.

AT THE CENTER OF THE UNIVERSE?

We know when the Big Bang took place. How about where? Seeing that everything is going away from us, does that mean that *this* point in space—where we are—is where it all happened?

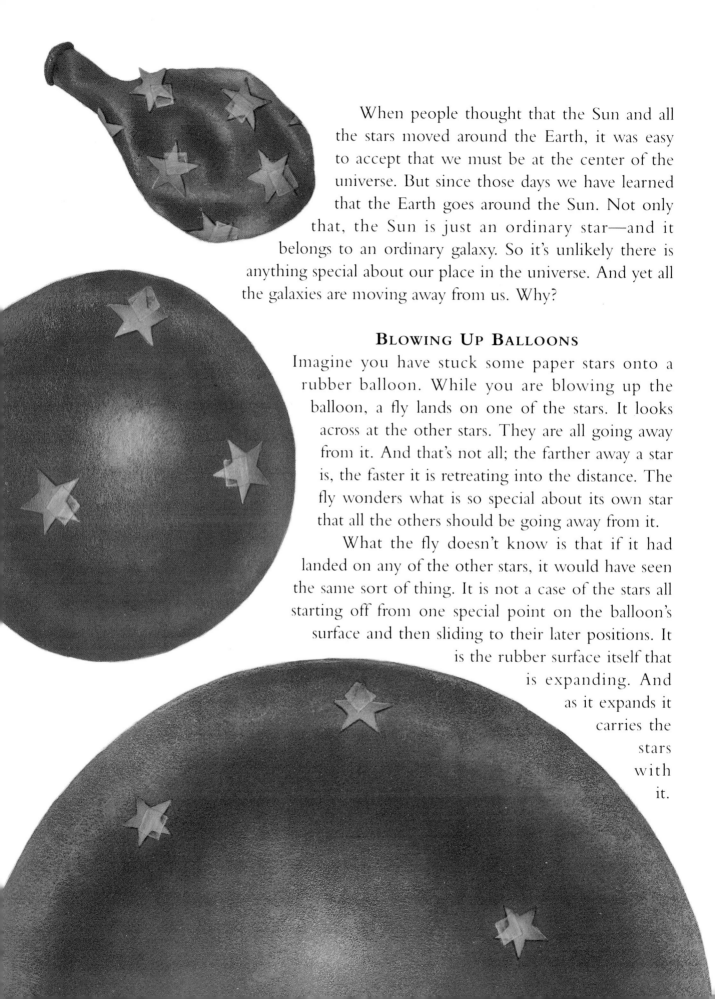

When people thought that the Sun and all the stars moved around the Earth, it was easy to accept that we must be at the center of the universe. But since those days we have learned that the Earth goes around the Sun. Not only that, the Sun is just an ordinary star—and it belongs to an ordinary galaxy. So it's unlikely there is anything special about our place in the universe. And yet all the galaxies are moving away from us. Why?

BLOWING UP BALLOONS

Imagine you have stuck some paper stars onto a rubber balloon. While you are blowing up the balloon, a fly lands on one of the stars. It looks across at the other stars. They are all going away from it. And that's not all; the farther away a star is, the faster it is retreating into the distance. The fly wonders what is so special about its own star that all the others should be going away from it.

What the fly doesn't know is that if it had landed on any of the other stars, it would have seen the same sort of thing. It is not a case of the stars all starting off from one special point on the balloon's surface and then sliding to their later positions. It is the rubber surface itself that is expanding. And as it expands it carries the stars with it.

THE BANG THAT HAPPENED EVERYWHERE

This gives us a way of understanding what is happening to the universe. It is not that all the matter starts off squashed together at one special point—which just happens to be where we live—with the rest of space empty. Nor does the matter then move outward from that point to fill up the rest of space. No. All the matter starts squashed up because *all of space starts squashed up* (just like the balloon was before being blown up). There was no other space outside this region. Then, with the Big Bang, space suddenly began to expand. As it did so, it carried the matter with it. So today, when we see distant galaxies moving away from us, it is because the space between us and those galaxies is expanding.

What would someone see from some other galaxy? The same thing: all the galaxies moving away from them. But that would not mean that they were at the center of the universe, any more than we are.

Expanding space? How can *nothing* expand? Strange to say, scientists often have to think of space as being something rather than nothing. A very smooth kind of something that can do things—it can affect whatever is in it. Odd, don't you think?

"The Big Bang happened here."

"No it didn't. The Big Bang happened here!"

Quiz

1. If a car has traveled 150 miles (240 km) at a steady speed of 50 mph (80 km/h), how long ago did it begin its journey?

2. Why would you expect the galaxies, as they fly apart, to be slowing down?

Answers on page 88

THE CREATION OF THE UNIVERSE

The Big Bang marks the beginning of the universe—the moment everything was created. At least, that is what most scientists think. If they are right, then it is important to find out as much as we can about it.

LOOKING BACK IN TIME

I have described one reason for believing there was a Big Bang: the galaxies are still moving apart after the explosion.

A second is this. When we look at distant galaxies, we are not seeing them as they are today. The light we are receiving set out on its long journey to us many years ago— in some cases, billions of years ago. So what we see now is how those galaxies were in the past. The farther away the galaxy, the farther back in time we see. And one of the things scientists find is that long ago galaxies were closer together than they are today. Which is good, because that is what we would expect if the universe really is expanding.

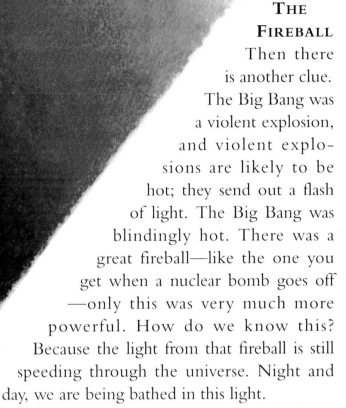

THE FIREBALL

Then there is another clue. The Big Bang was a violent explosion, and violent explosions are likely to be hot; they send out a flash of light. The Big Bang was blindingly hot. There was a great fireball—like the one you get when a nuclear bomb goes off —only this was very much more powerful. How do we know this? Because the light from that fireball is still speeding through the universe. Night and day, we are being bathed in this light.

But if that's so, where is it? After all, if you look up at the night sky, you don't exactly get blinded by light! No, but the light from the fireball has been on its journey to us ever since the Big Bang 15 billion years ago. In all that time, it has cooled down and slowly changed color: from yellow to orange to red to dull red, and finally to a "color" our eyes do not detect. We call it **microwave radiation**. What was once light energy has now become the sort of heat energy we cook with in microwave ovens! Although we cannot see it with our eyes, it can be picked up by a special kind of radio receiver.

This then is another reason for believing there was a Big Bang: we have detected its fireball.

★ ★ ★ ★ *1* ★ ★ ★ ★

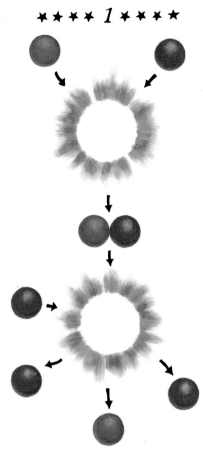

At first, if neutrons and protons fused to form a nucleus, they were quickly broken up again by other particles.

NUCLEAR COOKING

And there is yet another clue the Big Bang has left behind.

In the early stages of the Big Bang, everything was so violent that only the simplest kinds of particles could exist. Neutrons and protons might, from time to time, fuse together to form a bigger nucleus. But right away it got smashed into by some other particle, and was broken apart again. In the same way, an electron might briefly get together with a nucleus to form an atom. But this too could not last; the electron was easily knocked flying again. So at this stage there were only separate neutrons, protons, and electrons.

Later, the expansion thinned out the matter and things calmed down a bit. At this stage, when a bigger nucleus formed, there was less chance of it being hit by another particle—the other particles being too spread out. Not only that, the particles were not moving so fast now. So even if our newly formed nucleus did get hit, it would be a gentler hit, and the nucleus had a better chance of bouncing off without getting broken. Now some bigger nuclei could form.

★ ★ ★ ★ *2* ★ ★ ★ ★

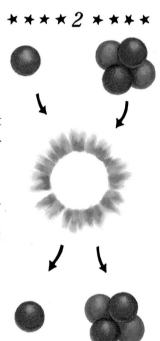

Later, bigger nuclei could survive the collisions.

But this did not last. Soon the particles had cooled down and thinned out so much that nuclear fusion stopped. No more nuclei were being formed; none were being broken up. The mixture of different-sized nuclei had become fixed.

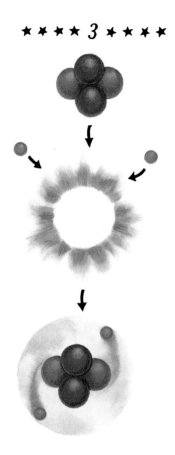

Electrons could now be captured by nuclei to form atoms.

Later still, electrons found themselves able to fasten onto these nuclei to form complete atoms; they could do this without getting knocked away again.

So, out of the Big Bang we ended up with a mixture of several kinds of atoms. But what mixture exactly? Well, it depends. It depends mostly on how densely packed the matter in the universe was: the more matter there was, the greater the chance of fusing together the bigger nuclei. By measuring how dense matter is today, and allowing for all the thinning out that has happened due to the expansion, scientists are able to figure out how dense it was at any point in the past. That in turn lets them work out what the mixture of atoms should have been.

Scientists figure that most of the stuff coming out of the Big Bang was probably the lightest gas, hydrogen. About a quarter of it was helium, and there were tiny amounts of other types of atoms.

And when scientists look at the gases out of which the stars form, what amounts do they actually find? Mostly hydrogen, a quarter helium, and not much else. It all works out brilliantly!

hydrogen

helium

the rest

STARTING AT THE BEGINNING (ALMOST!)

Having seen the evidence for the Big Bang, we can now start at the beginning and describe how the universe developed.

We cannot take our history of the world right back to the time zero when it all began. Why not? Because our present ideas tell us that, at that instant, all the matter in the universe was squashed down to an **infinite** density. There is no way our science can handle that! So science cannot say anything about the all-important instant of creation. Instead, we have to allow the universe to develop a bit before we can take up the story. And I do mean just "a bit". We can start our story once the universe is just a tiny fraction of a second old!

In the first few seconds we have high-speed neutrons, protons, and electrons banging around. Within a few minutes, nuclei form. Then, 100,000 years later, we get complete atoms. The gas expanding from the Big Bang is made up mostly of hydrogen atoms.

That is all there would ever be, a gradually thinning gas, except for one thing: in this gas there were places where, by chance, the density was a little higher than average. This higher density meant that these regions pulled on others with a slightly stronger gravity force than average. Gas was

drawn into these denser regions, making them even more dense and making their gravity force even stronger. That is how great swirling clouds began to form, the clouds out of which stars took shape.

One idea is that at first there were just a few very large clouds. These became clusters; the clusters then broke up into separate galaxies, and finally the galaxies broke up to form the stars.

Another idea is that the stars formed first. They then joined up to form galaxies, which later joined up to form clusters. At present no one can be really sure which way around it went. This is one of the big problems still to be worked out.

FROM SUPERNOVAE TO SOLAR SYSTEM

One thing we can be sure about: at this stage there were no planets. To have planets you need heavy atoms. For example, the core of the Earth is molten iron. Where did iron come from? We have already seen that nothing much came out of the Big Bang except hydrogen and helium.

The answer is that most of the nuclei of the heavier atoms were fused together in the cores of the first stars. When these stars came to the end of their lives, the newly made nuclei were thrown out into space by supernovae explosions. There they mixed with the surrounding gas. This mixture of gas and dust then collapsed to form more stars, which in their turn led to more explosions. At last, planets could also form—out of the dust that wasn't there for the first group of stars. And that's how the Solar System started to form. The rest of that story you already know.

★ ★ ★ ★ ★ ★ ★ ★ ★

Imagine the history of the universe squashed down so that the Big Bang happened 24 hours ago. On this scale, our Solar System was born 7 hours ago, the first humans just 30 seconds ago, and you yourself about half of one ten-thousandth of a second ago!

★ ★ ★ ★ ★ ★ ★ ★ ★

WHEN IS A QUESTION NOT A QUESTION?

One final point before we leave the subject of the Big Bang. We have seen how it marked the creation of all the energy and matter of the universe. But we have also seen how the movement of the galaxies away from one another is due to the expansion of space itself. Space started out from a dot. So, the Big Bang marked the creation of space too!

Even that is not the end of these wonderful marvels. Scientists have discovered a very close connection between space and time—so close you can't have one without the other. They are like two sides of a coin. This means that if there was no space before the Big Bang there was also no time!

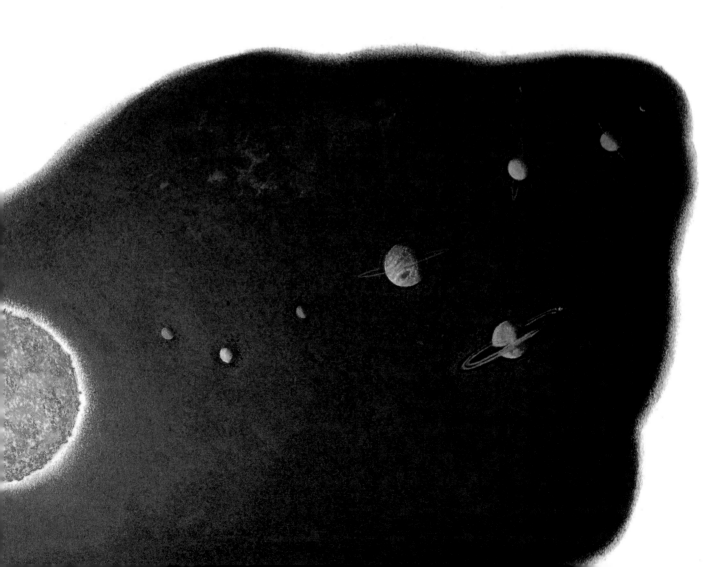

I am often asked, "What existed before the Big Bang?" I can't say. Why? It's not because I don't know the answer. It's because the question itself does not make sense. How could it? It talks about "before the Big Bang." But without any time then, there wasn't a "before"!

Some people who believe God created the world worry about this. If there was no Time before the moment of creation, how can we have a God who starts out on his own and then, *at some later point in time*, decides to make a world? We can't. Does that get rid of the idea of God? Some people think yes. I and others think no. The important thing about whether God is the Creator is not how he got things going in the first place, but "Why is there something, rather than nothing?" That still seems like a good question, for which one answer, perhaps the only answer, is "God".

"What existed before the Big Bang, Professor?"

Quiz

1. Suppose you are looking up at a star in the sky, and someone says to you, "That star might not actually be there anymore." What might they mean by that?

2. Remembering what we discovered in Chapter 10 about there being no special point in space where the Big Bang happened, where in the sky would you expect the microwave radiation to be coming from?

3. Carbon is an important type of atom for building plants and the bodies of animals and humans. Where did the carbon in your body come from in the first place?

Answers on pages 88–89

THE FUTURE OF THE UNIVERSE

★·★·★·★·★·★·★·★·★·★·★

Will the galaxies escape gravity's grip?

★·★·★·★·★·★·★·★·★·★·★

Having looked to the past to see how everything began, and how the universe came to be the way it is today, it is now time to look to the future. What does cosmology have to say about how the universe will develop from here on?

PULLING IN ALL DIRECTIONS

We have seen how the galaxies are still moving away from one another as the universe expands. But we also know that the expansion must be slowing down. Why? Because our own Galaxy's gravity force stretches out into space, pulling on all the other galaxies. This pull tends to slow them down. And the same is true of all the other galaxies; they are all pulling on one another with gravity, trying to hold one another back.

As the galaxies get farther apart, these gravity forces become less and less. The galaxies are slowing down, but the braking force that makes them slow down is getting weaker by the day. The Big Question then becomes this: are the gravity forces strong enough to stop the galaxies before they can get completely away, or are the galaxies moving so fast that they will escape gravity's grip?

Answer that question, and you will know the future of the universe.

FREEZING TO DEATH

If gravity loses this battle, then the expansion of the universe will go on forever.

For a while, new stars will continue to form and live out their lives. But there will come a time when there is no more nuclear fuel to burn; it will all have been used up. The last of the stars will die; they will end up as the cooled-down remains of white dwarfs, or neutron stars, or black holes. All life on the planets will come to an end. Everything will become freezing cold. This is called the **heat death** of the universe.

What will happen after that? We can't be sure. But one bet is that everything in a galaxy might, in time, get gobbled up into one enormous black hole at the center of the galaxy. This black hole might then join up with the black hole remains of the other galaxies belonging to the same cluster—to form an even bigger black hole.

Whatever the details might be, the outlook seems pretty bleak. Not that it is anything for us to worry about. We shall all be dead and gone long, long before any of this is due to take place!

CRUNCHING AND BOUNCING

But what if gravity is strong enough to halt the galaxies in their tracks? What happens then?

The gravity forces are still pulling. So no sooner do the galaxies stop than they start to be pulled together again; they begin moving in the opposite direction. As time goes by, they pick up speed.

The same thing would happen to the stars stuck to that balloon on page 62 if you now let the air out. . . .

"I'm cold! Is this what they mean by the heat death?"

Black holes just love frozen stars!

While this is happening, the microwave radiation from the Big Bang fireball (which is still rushing around) finds that the universe is getting smaller. As the radiation squashes down, it heats up and changes "color" again until it becomes visible once more. The sky becomes red, and then turns orange, yellow, white. . . .

In the end, all the matter and all the radiation in the universe will come crashing together. We call this spectacular pile-up the **Big Crunch**!

What then? Well, that might be it—the end of everything—the end of the universe—it simply goes out of existence.

But then again, perhaps not. One suggestion is that after the Big Crunch, there would be a **Big Bounce**. All the matter would come expanding out again. If that's right, then perhaps what we have been calling the Big Bang was just the latest Big Bounce. How many bounces were there before that? Who knows? Perhaps the universe uas been bouncing forever; perhaps the universe never had a beginning, and will have no end!

THE $64,000 QUESTION

So, what's it to be? An ever-expanding freeze, or a hot crunch?

The answer depends on how strong the gravity force is. That in turn depends on how much matter there is producing the gravity force. What we have to do is figure out the density of matter in the universe. We take a typical region of space and add up all the matter in it. If the density is more than a certain amount (called the **critical value**), gravity will be strong enough, one day, to stop the expansion and bring it all back together in a Big Crunch.

On the other hand, if the density is *less* than critical, the expansion will go on forever.

So, what could be easier? Let's start counting!

We add up all the matter in the stars and in the gas and dust between the stars. The result? A density that is only one hundredth of the critical value. So, that's it. There is not enough matter to stop the galaxies. The expansion goes on for ever.

Except wait! A recount has been demanded!

THE INVISIBLE UNIVERSE

When we were talking about galaxies in Chapter 9, I described how the outer stars were whirling around the center of the Galaxy too fast for them to be held in orbit by the gravity of the inner stars. It only made sense if there was matter in the Galaxy that we did not see—"dark matter." And, if you remember, there was a lot of it—ten times as much as the matter we do see. It is the dark matter that really holds the stars of the Galaxy together. So all that dark matter has to be added to our list. When we do that, the density becomes one tenth of the critical value—not the one-hundredth we came up with before.

And even that is not the end of it. That simply takes care of the dark matter inside galaxies. Could there be dark matter *outside* the galaxies?

Actually, when we look at how the galaxies in a cluster of galaxies move around one another, there is a hint that there might well be extra dark matter in the spaces between them. How much? It's difficult to say —but again it could be a lot. And finally, there could be yet more of the stuff outside the cluster, holding the supercluster together. In fact, altogether, the density might turn out to be very close to the critical value!

Weighing all the visible matter...

Adding all the dark matter that's inside the galaxies...

Adding all the dark matter that's outside the galaxies.

SEEING THE UNSEEN

In the story of the Invisible Man, how could people tell when he was around? By his clothes and the bandages wrapped around his face. From what people could see, and the way those things moved around, they could figure out where the man must be, even though they could not see him directly.

That is how it is with the dark matter in the universe. By studying the stars and galaxies, and the way they move, we can figure out where the invisible dark matter must be.

HOW EMBARRASSING!

What actually is this dark matter? What is it made of?

Some scientists think it might be neutrinos; others say it might be some unknown, "exotic" matter left over from the Big Bang—matter that we do not find in our normal atomic matter. Or it might be a mixture of the two. Frankly, we don't know. Imagine not knowing what ninety-nine percent of the universe is made of!

"What exactly is dark matter, Professor?"

"Er, um . . ."

SOMETHING FISHY

For all we know, the density of the universe could have been billions or trillions of times more than—or less than—the critical value. The fact that it comes out so close to the critical value is very odd. Is it just a coincidence?

Scientists think not. They suspect that something happened immediately after the instant of the Big Bang to make sure the density got that value. In fact, they now think they know how it happened. When the Universe was just a tiny, tiny fraction of a second old, it went through a special type of super-fast expansion called **inflation**. One of the interesting things about inflation is that scientists think it would automatically force the density to be critical.

AND THE FINAL RESULT IS...

So, after all that, what is going to happen to the universe?

If the density really is critical, then the expansion will slow down to a mere crawl, and then, way off in the infinite future, it will just about come to a halt. In the meantime, the universe will have suffered a heat death—just as it would if the density were *less* than critical and the expansion went on forever.

But having the critical density depends on the inflation idea being correct. It's a red-hot topic at the moment. You will have to watch your newspapers for the latest on that!

★ ★ ★ ★ ★ ★ ★ ★ ★

Scientists think that inflation lasted for only a tiny fraction of a second. During that time, the universe suddenly swelled from an infinitesimally small dot to the size of a grapefruit. Now it had critical density.

The universe kept on growing—just a moment later, it was the size of our Sun.

★ ★ ★ ★ ★ ★ ★ ★ ★

Quiz

1. Someone says to you, "In a Big Crunch, all the matter disappears, leaving behind only empty space." Do you agree? If not, what would you say to set them straight?

2. Why do you think it is impossible for science to figure out what would happen after a Big Crunch? (Hint: remember what I said about why science cannot talk about the actual instant of the Big Bang.)

3. At the end of Chapter 11 we said there was no time before the Big Bang. But if there were to be a Big Crunch, can you see how what we said then might be wrong?

Answers on page 89

AN UNFRIENDLY UNIVERSE, OR IS IT ?

I have now finished sharing with you what I know about the universe. It is time for our imaginary spaceship to take us home. But first I would like to add a few thoughts about what all this might mean. What does it tell us about living creatures, about you and me?

WHERE DO WE FIT IN?

I can well imagine how you are feeling. It is a bit unsettling to learn that the Earth is just an ordinary planet, going around an ordinary star, in an ordinary galaxy; that there are 10 sextillion (10×10^{21}) other stars; that the universe is already 200 million times older than you and I will ever be; that because the universe is so huge some of the light that started out on its journey at the Big Bang has only just reached us; that most of our Sun's planets are such horrid places no one could possibly live there; that the Earth itself will one day be burned to ashes when the Sun swells up to be a red giant; that the universe will end up frozen and completely lifeless.

It sounds like such an unfriendly universe, don't you think? No wonder some people, when they learn about these things, get to thinking that the development of life on Earth through **evolution** must be just an accident—a freak of nature.

The Goldilocks Factor

But wait! It's not as simple as that. . . .

NOT TOO LITTLE, NOT TOO MUCH

The Big Bang was violent—frighteningly so. But what a good thing it was so powerful. Why? Well, if it had gone off more gently, the matter would not have been thrown out as fast. Gravity would then have pulled it all back together again in a Big Crunch—and this could have happened before there had been chance for life to develop. Remember, the universe had to keep going for 15 billion years before we humans appeared on Earth. And that meant the universe had to keep expanding for all that time. That in turn meant it had to end up huge. In fact, in order for there to be life, it could not have been smaller. As I said, thank goodness the Big Bang was BIG!

But careful! It also had to be not too big. If the Big Bang had been more violent it would have blown everything apart too fast. Then the hydrogen and helium gas would not have been able to gather together to form the clouds which were later to become stars and planets. No stars or planets, no life.

too big

too small

So, the Big Bang had to walk a narrow tightrope between being too violent, and not being violent enough. It could not vary much either way. Luckily for us, it turned out just right.

just right

NOT TOO WEAK, NOT TOO STRONG

Having got the violence of the Big Bang right so that clouds of gas could form, the next question is: What size are the clouds going to be? After all, we know that if we are to have a star, there is a certain minimum amount of gas that has to collect together. Below that limit, the temperature rise is not enough to light the nuclear fire, and we end up with a brown dwarf.

★ ★ ★ ★ ★ ★ ★ ★ ★

too strong

too weak

just right

★ ★ ★ ★ ★ ★ ★ ★ ★

If the gravity force had been weaker than it actually was, all the clouds of gas would have been smaller. In that case, there might well have been no true stars—only "failed stars" like Jupiter. Again: no stars, no life.

On the other hand, if gravity had been stronger, the clouds would have been bigger. "What's wrong with that?" you might ask. The trouble is that the bigger the cloud, the bigger and brighter the star. We have seen how a star much above 50 to 100 times as massive as the Sun is so hot that the light it gives out pushes the extra gas away. And the star that is left burns itself out in only a tiny fraction of the time that the Sun takes. So, if you have only big stars, there is not enough time for life to develop on any neighboring planets before the star blows up as a supernova.

What a good thing that gravity was neither too weak nor too strong!

KEEPING THE FIRE GOING

Why is it important to have the Sun burning for a long time? Because it takes a long, long time for life to develop.

Scientists believe that we human beings evolved from the same ancestors as the apes; and these ancestors came from simpler forms of life; and these in their turn came from even simpler forms; and so on, right back to the "dirt" or matter that the Earth is made of! As you can imagine, this took a long, long time. In fact, it has been going on ever since the Earth formed, 4.6 billion years ago.

During all that time there had to be a steady source of energy to keep things going. As we saw in Chapter 3, that source of energy is the Sun, the nuclear bomb that goes off very, very slowly.

There is something quite remarkable going on here. On the one hand, there is the strength of the gravity force, which controls how much gas (in other words, fuel) is fed into the fire. On the other hand, there is the rate at which nuclear fusion takes place, which controls how fast the nuclear fire burns. Now, as far as we know, these are two quite different things—no connection between them. And yet, amazingly, they seem to be in tune with each other; they work together to produce a range of slow-burning stars, like the Sun, which are needed for life to develop. We strike it lucky again!

THREE INTO ONE WON'T GO, OR WILL IT?

It is all very well saying that we evolved from "dirt," but where did the dirt come from in the first place? In particular, we need to know where carbon comes from. Carbon is a very "sticky" kind of atom, important for gluing together the complicated atomic structures in our bodies.

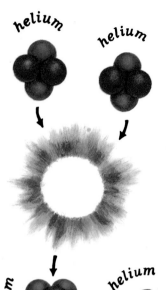

We have already learned that carbon is made from nuclear fusion taking place in the cores of stars. But there is a problem. To make carbon, we need three helium nuclei to bang into one another and fuse. That is very tricky. Playing billiards, it is easy to get two balls to collide. But three, all at the same time? For the same reason it would seem impossible to make carbon. And yet, somehow, stars managed to do it. How?

What we find is this: if two helium nuclei bang into each other, they can sometimes stick together for a short while to form a beryllium nucleus. If a third helium nucleus comes along, it can fuse with this pair before it splits up. Unfortunately, the first two stay together for only a tiny, tiny fraction of a second. So that doesn't solve the problem. We need something else.

One of the strange things about nuclei is that when two of them collide, their apparent size depends on how fast they approach each other. It turns out that at the sort of speeds found in a star, the beryllium nucleus appears absolutely enormous to the approaching helium nucleus! They have no difficulty banging into each other and fusing to form carbon. Yet another stroke of luck!

ESCAPE FROM ALCATRAZ

It is said that no one ever escaped from the prison on the island of Alcatraz. But trying to get away from there was nothing compared with the problem now facing the newly made carbon. There it is, stuck in the middle of a large star. No way can life develop in the middle of a star, so somehow it has to get out. But how? You already know the answer to that: when the star burns out and collapses in on itself, the carbon and other materials get blasted out in the supernova explosion.

But that's odd, isn't it? Something that is collapsing *inwards* produces something that is thrown *outward*? And if we think a blast of ghostly neutrinos did it, isn't that even

stranger? Suppose these slippery particles had been just a wee bit more slippery and had left the carbon behind?

A LAST-MINUTE RUSH

Not only that, something else extraordinary happens in supernovae explosions. Not all the kinds of atoms we find on Earth are present in the star before the explosion takes place. So where do they come from? The answer is that they are made during the explosion itself! That's right. It's as though the star thinks to itself, "Whoops! I forgot to make some so-and-so; they'll be needing that." And does it at the last minute as everything is on its way out.

SO, WHAT ARE WE TO MAKE OF IT?

Even that is not the end of the list of "coincidences." But I think enough has already been said to show that the universe, far from being unfriendly to us, seems to have bent over backward to make it possible for us to be here. But why?

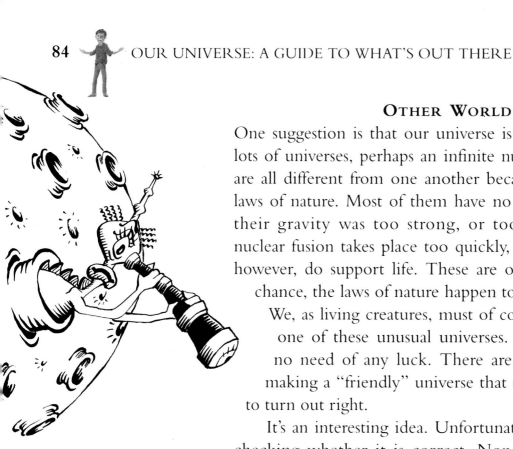

OTHER WORLDS

One suggestion is that our universe is not alone. There are lots of universes, perhaps an infinite number of them! They are all different from one another because each has its own laws of nature. Most of them have no life in them. Perhaps their gravity was too strong, or too weak; perhaps the nuclear fusion takes place too quickly, or too slowly. A few, however, do support life. These are ones where, purely by chance, the laws of nature happen to allow life to develop.

We, as living creatures, must of course find ourselves in one of these unusual universes. Which means there's no need of any luck. There are so many attempts at making a "friendly" universe that one of them is bound to turn out right.

It's an interesting idea. Unfortunately, there's no way of checking whether it is correct. None of the universes, if they are there, would actually be able to get in touch with one another.

SOMEONE'S FIXED IT?

Another suggestion is that there is only one universe, and it has been deliberately designed to be a home for life. That is what some religious people believe. They hold that God created the universe as a place where he could bring into existence living creatures—not just human beings on planet Earth, but life wherever it develops. Again, no luck is involved. It was *meant* to be that way.

OVER TO YOU

I myself go along with the second of these suggestions; I believe that from the very start the universe was planned to be our special home. I can't prove it, of course. It is something you will have to decide for yourself. And that's another journey.

Final Quiz

1. Which do you think is the most reasonable explanation of our "friendly" universe?

 a) Sheer fluke.

 b) There are lots of different universes, so one was bound to be like ours.

 c) God designed it to be that way.

2. Which of these unsolved problems do you hope the next generation of scientists will solve first?

 a) Why the galaxies are arranged like a gigantic sponge.

 b) Whether the galaxies formed first and then joined up to make clusters, or whether the clusters came first and then separated into galaxies.

 c) The nature of dark matter.

 d) How much dark matter there is.

 e) The long-term future of the universe.

 f) What happened at the very instant of the Big Bang.

 g) What would happen after a Big Crunch.

 h) Whether there is life on Saturn's moon, Titan.

 i) Whether there is life elsewhere in the universe.

*Sorry. This is one quiz for which
I don't have the answers!*

Quiz Answers

CHAPTER 1

1. **a)** The Earth is round, not flat.

   b) There is no special direction in space called "down".

   c) The Sun and stars do not go around the Earth; it is the Earth that spins. (You might also have mentioned that the sky is not a hollow dome with twinkly lights on it, and that atoms are mostly empty space, and not solid.)

2. You can never get completely away from Earth's gravity. As it says on page 6, gravity forces stretch to infinity (though they do become very, very weak).

3. As it says on page 9, each different type of atom has a different size nucleus, as well as different numbers of electrons.

CHAPTER 2

1. A feather, a brick, a human body, in fact anything at all, will weigh less on the Moon. This is because the Moon does not pull as strongly as the Earth. It has nothing to do with being slim.

2. Everything pulls on everything else with gravity. So the Moon's gravity does pull on the Earth. In fact, this is what causes the tides; water in the seas and oceans moves this way and that way in response to the Moon's pull.

CHAPTER 3

1. If you look at the picture on page 18, you'll see that during spring and fall the Earth's axis is pointing neither toward nor away from the Sun. So the weather is "in-between" type weather.

2. Nuclear fusion needs a high temperature to start. On page 19, we saw that the temperature in the middle of the Sun is 27 million degrees. How can we get a temperature that high? And if we succeed, how are we going to hold something together that is so hot? Any box we put it in would melt! The Sun doesn't need a box. It holds everything together by gravity. Scientists are trying to do it with magnetic forces.

3. How much you weigh on the Sun or the Moon or the Earth depends on how much mass they have. It also depends on how far you are from their center when you stand on their surface. The Sun has 333,000 times the mass of the Earth, which would make you weigh more. But the Sun's diameter is 109 times bigger, so you'd be farther from its center, and that would tend to make you weigh less. In the end, the extra mass wins out. In fact, you would weigh 28 times as much on the Sun as on the Earth. (Not that you would notice—you'd be too frizzled!)

CHAPTER 4

1. It takes one Earth-year for the Earth to go around the Sun, and 248 Earth-years for far-off Pluto to do it. In general, the farther out from the Sun a planet is, the farther it has to go and the longer it takes. Jupiter is farther than Mercury, so its "year" is longer (nearly 12 Earth-years compared to Mercury's 88 Earth-days).

2. Jupiter is farther from the Sun than Earth is, so you would expect its moon, Ganymede, to be colder than our Moon.

CHAPTER 5

1. Neither Mercury nor the Moon has an atmosphere. That means they have no weather! There are no rains or winds to wear down the craters. On the Earth, most of our craters have been covered up or worn away by now.

2. The whole Solar System started out as a single cloud of gas and dust that was slowly spinning around an axis. Part of this cloud collapsed to the center where it became the Sun, which continued to spin on the original axis; the rest of the cloud became a disk which also continued to rotate in the same direction. The disk then broke up into planets, which carried on the same rotation.

CHAPTER 6

1. They look tiny because all stars, except for the Sun, are so very far away.

2. In Chapter 5, we saw how Jupiter almost became a sun, but not quite. This was because it did not get hot enough to trigger its nuclear fire. But having looked around the stars, we now know there are lots of these failed stars. We call them brown dwarfs. So, that is what Jupiter is—a brown dwarf.

CHAPTER 7

1. You read on page 20 that the Sun formed 4.6 billion years ago. It won't become a red giant for another 5 billion years. So that means the Sun is about halfway through its life as a normal star. (After that it becomes a red giant, but that will only add on another tenth to its active life.)

2. The right order is **b, c, d, a**—going from the youngest to the oldest.

CHAPTER 8

1. 50-100 times as massive. As I said on page 44, stars cannot be much bigger than that. Any extra matter gets blown away as soon as the star brightens up.

2. A white dwarf. The question is a bit tricky. The star spends most of its life twice as massive as the Sun, which is more than the one and a half times needed to become a neutron star. But it loses matter when it becomes a giant. To *end up* with one and a half times the Sun's mass, a star has to begin with about eight times that. (See page 49.)

3. a) Electron "soup".
   b) Neutron "soup".
   c) Nothing; the outer layers, like the rest of the star, squash down to a point.

4. The beam is steady. However, like that of a lighthouse, looks as though it is being switched on and off because of the way it swings around to point in our direction, and then away from us.

5. The horizon is the limit of how far you can see on a clear day. The "horizon" of a black hole is the limit of how far you can see into a black hole. Light from farther in cannot get out to you.

6. You cannot signal home. Nothing at all can get out of a black hole.

CHAPTER 9

1. Black holes can form **a)** when a heavy star ends its life and collapses in on itself, and **b)** from the matter that ends up at the center of a galaxy.

2. "Dark matter" is not another name for matter that has fallen into a black hole. It is the name given to all the matter in the galaxy we cannot see. Whereas one million stars out of the 100 billion of our Galaxy might be in a black hole at the center, dark matter amounts to *ten times* as much as all the visible stars.

3. It is gravity that holds the galaxies together in groups and clusters. Although the galaxies are far from one another, their gravity reaches out into *all* of space.

CHAPTER 10

1. At 50 mph (80 km/h), it would take three hours to travel 150 miles (240 km). So that's how long ago it is since the car set out. This is the same kind of sum we have to do to figure out how long ago it was since the matter in the universe started out from the Big Bang.

2. The galaxies are all pulling on one another with gravity forces, and these tend to slow the galaxies down. This slowing down makes it a bit more difficult to figure out when the Big Bang happened. Are these forces strong enough to bring the galaxies to a stop one day? I shall talk about that in Chapter 12.

CHAPTER 11

1. They mean that it has taken a long time for the light you are now seeing to get here. In all that time, the star itself might have disappeared; it might have blown itself up in a supernova explosion.

2. The Big Bang did not happen at any one special place in space; it happened *everywhere*. That means the fireball happened everywhere. So we expect its light (the microwave radiation) to be coming to us equally from all directions. And that is indeed what we find.

3. Very little except hydrogen and helium came from the Big Bang. So the carbon in your body must have been made by fusion of hydrogen and helium in the core of a star, a star that later blew up as a supernova explosion and threw the carbon out into space. From there it collected together to form planet Earth, and then you!

CHAPTER 12

1. They've got it wrong. Everything comes back together again because it is space itself that is squashing down. So at the instant of the Big Crunch, space disappears along with all the matter.

2. At the instant of the Big Crunch, the density of matter becomes infinite, and science cannot deal with that. It was the same with that first instant of the Big Bang.

3. If after a Big Crunch you get a Big Bounce, and the Big Bang was just the latest in a series of Big Bounces, then there *would* have been time before the Big Bang, time during which all the other bounces were taking places.

★★★★★★★★★★★★ # Glossary ★★★★★★★★★★★★★★

OF SCIENTIFIC WORDS AND THEIR MEANINGS

angular momentum A property of spinning bodies that depends on how fast they spin, how heavy they are, and their shape and size. If the size is reduced, for example, when a spinning star shrinks, then it has to spin faster to keep the same angular momentum.

asteroids Thousands of rocks and minor planets orbiting the Sun between Mars and Jupiter.

atmosphere The layers of gas surrounding a planet, held by gravity.

atom An atom has a central nucleus surrounded by electrons. Most matter is made up of just 92 different types of atoms, each with a different number of electrons and a different size of nucleus.

Big Bang The idea that at some time in the past (about 15 billion years ago) all the matter of the universe, and all of space itself, was squashed up with infinite density; it then expanded violently and rapidly. It is thought that the Big Bang marked the creation of the universe.

Big Bounce The possibility that if the universe suffers a Big Crunch, it might then bounce and expand again.

Big Crunch The possibility that one day the expansion of the universe will stop, and that everything will come rushing back together and squash down again to infinite density.

binary stars Two stars held close together by gravity and moving around each other.

black hole A black hole is formed when matter is unable to hold itself up against its own gravity force. All the matter ends up at a point, and this point is surrounded by very powerful gravity forces. Black holes are believed to be formed when very massive old stars die, and also when matter concentrates at the center of a galaxy.

blue giant An old, massive star that has swelled to an even larger size and whose outer layers are so hot that they glow with a bluish color.

brown dwarf A brown dwarf is formed when a collapsing cloud fails to heat up enough to trigger off the nuclear fusion needed to produce a proper star. This happens when the cloud does not have enough matter in it.

carbon Carbon is a type of atom especially important for making plants and the bodies of animals and humans. It is itself made by nuclear fusion in the cores of stars, and later blasted out of the star by a supernova explosion.

cluster A collection of galaxies held together by their gravity forces. Groups of clusters can form superclusters.

comets Dirty balls of ice that orbit the Sun, usually a long way off. When they get in close, however, they heat up and give off gases that reflect the sunlight and often form a bright "tail".

constellation A pattern formed by those stars that happen to lie in roughly the same direction in the sky. The stars are usually at very different distances from us, so they don't really have anything to do with one another.

cosmology The study of the content, behavior, history, and future of the universe as a whole.

critical value The amount of density that matter in the universe would have to have in order to stop the expansion of the universe at some time in the infinite future.

dark matter Matter in the universe that cannot be seen, but we suspect to be there from the behavior of the visible matter. Ninety percent of a galaxy seems to be dark matter, and as much as 99 percent of all the matter of the universe. At present no one can be sure what dark matter is made of.

density Density is mass divided by volume or size. It depends on how tightly packed something is. For example, if a cloud of gas with a certain mass squashed down to a smaller size, its density would increase.

dwarf stars Small-sized stars.

electron A tiny basic particle that is usually found in the outer part of an atom.

evolution (of humans) The idea that humans developed or evolved from the same ancestors as the apes, and they in turn evolved from yet simpler life forms, and the simpler forms originally evolved from non-living "dirt"!

expansion of the universe Distant galaxies are seen to be moving away from each other; the farther away the galaxy, the faster it is moving. This is because, ever since the Big Bang, space itself has been expanding.

galaxy A collection of about 100 billion stars, held together by gravity, and slowly rotating around its center. There are about 100 billion galaxies altogether in the universe. The Sun belongs to one we call the Galaxy (with a capital "G").

giant stars Old stars that have begun to run out of fuel and whose outer layers have swollen up enormously. Medium-sized stars, like the Sun, become red giants; more massive stars burn hotter and become blue giants.

gravity Everything pulls on everything else with a gravity force. The more matter there is, the stronger the force. There is no limit to how far it stretches out into space, but the greater the distance, the weaker the pull.

heat death The idea that in the distant future all the nuclear fuel in the universe will be used up, there will be no more stars, and the universe will become cold and lifeless.

helium The second lightest type of atom. It is usually in the form of a gas. Helium nuclei made up 25 percent of the visible matter coming out of the Big Bang. More are being made by the fusion of hydrogen nuclei in the cores of stars.

horizon (of a black hole) The horizon is an imaginary boundary surrounding the point at which all the matter of a black hole is concentrated. Anything that comes inside the horizon cannot escape being sucked into that point – not even light.

hydrogen The lightest type of atom. It is usually in the form of a gas. Hydrogen nuclei made up 75 percent of the visible matter coming out of the Big Bang.

infinite The biggest number that anyone can think of, and then a whole lot more added to it!

inflation The idea that a short time of extremely rapid expansion in the universe's early history produced a density that had critical value.

Local Group The name given to a group of about 30 galaxies to which our own Galaxy belongs.

mass This tells you how much "stuff" there is in an object—in particular, how hard it would be to push around.

"merry-go-round" force If no force acts on an object, it will stay still or continue moving steadily in a straight line. To get it to go in a circle, you have to pull on it sideways. I like to call this the "merry-go-round" force. (Its proper name is "centripetal" force.) With the planets, it takes all the Sun's gravity force to provide the "merry-go-round" needed force to keep the planets curving around in an orbit. There's no gravity left over to pull the planets any closer to the Sun. That's how they stay at a safe distance.

meteor A streak of light that flashes across the sky, sometimes called "a shooting star." It is caused by a meteoroid burning up on entry into the Earth's atmosphere.

meteorite A meteoroid that has survived passing through the Earth's atmosphere and has landed on the surface of the Earth as a rock.

meteoroids Small lumps of matter orbiting the Sun. If one of them meets up with a planet or moon, and doesn't get burned up in the atmosphere, it can cause a crater as it hits the surface. A meteoroid that successfully reaches the planet's surface is then called a meteorite.

microwave radiation The cooled-down remains of the fireball from the Big Bang. The radiation is coming to us equally from all parts of the sky.

Milky Way The faintly glowing, broad band of light that stretches across the night sky. This light is given out by the other stars of our Galaxy, as we look along the disk of the Galaxy.

moons Large rocky bodies that orbit planets. The Earth has one Moon; some of the other planets of the Solar System have several.

neutrino A tiny basic particle that hardly ever knocks into anything else. In spite of this, so many of them are produced when a massive star collapses that neutrinos are thought to be responsible for causing supernovae explosions.

neutron One of the two types of basic particles from which atomic nuclei are made—the other being the proton.

neutron star The dense, squashed-down remains of certain massive stars that have collapsed in on themselves at the end of their lives. It is a couple of miles across and is made of neutrons.

nuclear energy, nuclear fuel, and nuclear fusion If nuclei hit each other hard enough, they can sometimes fuse together to form a larger nucleus. In some cases, energy is given out. This nuclear energy is what powers the Sun and other stars.

nucleus The central part of an atom.

orbit The path taken by one object around another—for example, the Earth going around the Sun, or the Moon around the Earth. They are in the form of ellipses, although some ellipses are almost circles.

planets The nine major objects orbiting the Sun. It is thought likely that other stars will also have planets.

proton The nucleus of a hydrogen atom. It is also one of the two types of basic particles from which other atomic nuclei are made—the other being the neutron.

pulsar A star from which we receive a rapid and regular series of radio pulses. Pulsars are now believed to be fast-spinning neutron stars. They emit radio waves in a beam that is actually steady, but because it is swept around the sky it is not always pointing in our direction, and so appears to be pulsing on and off.

red dwarf A small star that does not get as hot as other stars, and so glows red.

red giant An old star that has swelled to a large size and whose outer layers are quite cool and so glow red.

rings Several planets are surrounded by thin disks of orbiting dust and bits of ice, called rings. Saturn is particularly famous for its rings.

Solar System The name given to the Sun, its planets, and everything else that orbits around it.

star "True" stars are those condensed clouds of gas that have heated up enough to trigger a nuclear fire. The name "star," however, can also describe other bodies that are not powered by nuclear fusion but still emit radiation—for example, brown dwarfs and neutron stars.

Sun Our local star. As an ordinary medium

-sized star, it is roughly halfway through its active life.

supernova explosion The explosion that happens when a massive star nears the end of its active life. While its core collapses, its outer parts are blasted away —probably by neutrinos.

universe Usually this means the whole of time and space and matter. But if we happen to be thinking of the universe as possibly being one of many universes, then "the universe" means the time, space, and matter that might affect us; we can never have contact with anything belonging to other universes.

white dwarf The leftover remains of a medium-sized star. The Sun is expected to end its active life as a white dwarf.

★ ★ ★ ★ ★ ★ ★ ★ ★ ★ ★ ★ ★ ★ ★ # Index ★ ★ ★ ★ ★ ★ ★ ★ ★ ★ ★ ★ ★ ★ ★

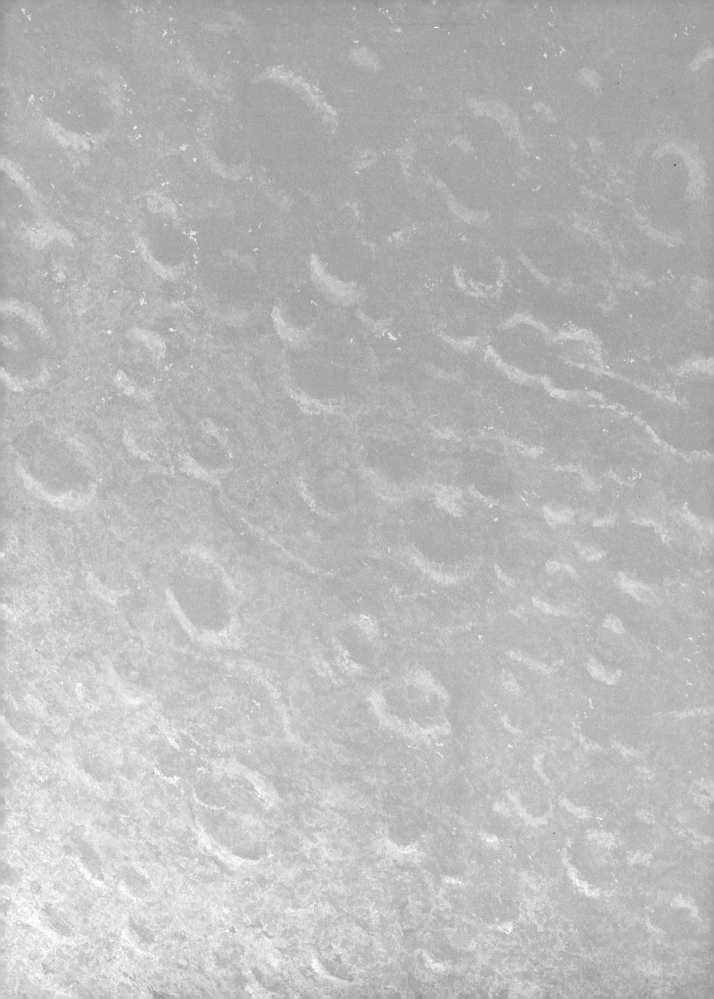